The Secret of TRANSITIONS

How to Move Effortlessly to Higher Levels of Success

by

Jim Manton

Robert D. Reed Publishers • Bandon, OR

Robert D. Reed Publishers
P.O. Box 1992
Bandon, OR 97411
Phone: 541-347-9882 • Fax: -9883
E-mail: 4bobreed@msn.com
web site: www.rdrpublishers.com

Cover Designer: **Cleone Lyvonne**
Typesetter: **Barbara Kruger**

ISBN 978-1-931741-91-0

Library of Congress Control Number 2007934875

Manufactured, typeset and printed in the United States of America

DEDICATION

For
Patsy, Cory, Jenny and Molly

ACKNOWLEDGMENTS

To Patsy for the love that she is.

To my clients for their courage, commitment and trust…and especially for what they teach me about myself.

To the women business owners who amaze me with their incredible capacity to lead and make a difference not only at work, but also in the community and at home.

To Steve Chandler for his guidance, support, inspiration, and creative vision.

To Steve Hardison for seeing it wasn't success that was missing but rather an open heart.

To Jim and Gindy Myers for the helping hand and knowing exactly when to let go.

To Jane Lance for confronting my hubris.

To Kathy Chandler for her editing and encouragement.

To Joseph Campbell and Alan Watts for their wisdom.

To Byron Katie for loving what is.

CONTENTS

THE CALL UNANSWERED

"Often in actual life, and not infrequently in popular tales, you encounter the dull case of the call unanswered; for it is always possible to turn an ear to other self interests.

Refusal of the summons converts the adventure into its negative. Walled in boredom and hard work, the subject loses the power to take significant affirmative action and becomes a victim to be saved."

Joseph Campbell

You look in a mirror and see something for the first time—a gray hair, a wrinkle or a bag under the eye. You look even deeper and see that love is gone, that business is bad, or that you truly are underachieving. You feel distant from what was once captivating.

You are jarred by the sudden awareness of discontent. Backs ache. Waists expand. The once healthy and vibrant find themselves feeling stressed and sick. Achievers reach their goals and plateau. What was challenging becomes routine and predictable. You've let boredom settle in where you were once energized and engaged.

Other times it is a messenger that wakes us up. A banker, a doctor, a boss, a peer, a friend or a loved one has the courage to tell us the truth. The message is clear. You are challenged to change or risk losing a relationship or perhaps a significant opportunity. Sometimes it takes more than that, it takes a traumatic event—the loss of a loved one, divorce, a serious illness, a life-threatening injury, a business failure or a major financial loss. Whatever it is that awakens us, it is a calling, a summons to act.

We all realize that everything is in a state of constant change. We just don't see or feel it as it occurs. It's only after a significant amount of change has accumulated that we begin to have a sense of contrast. So we often see our lives unfolding as a series of relative stable periods separated by distinct events and milestones. These events wake us up and we start to notice.

Waking up and seeing clearly is the beginning of transition, a point of departure—the ending of the old and familiar, and the beginning of the new and unexplored. Births, deaths, marriage, divorce, promotion, or termination. We never forget these moments. The emotional impact of a major transition burns itself into a lifelong memory.

If you are an adult, you have already experienced several significant transitions. You may recall having a sense of discontent and restlessness that signaled an approaching transition. Was that discontent a powerful motivator or a setback? You may have found that you're at your best when you are dissatisfied with the status quo. But often people find that they are not ready to move on, so they search for new ways to revitalize their efforts and keep things going. But keeping things going can be a fatal error. This is Campbell's warning about not answering the call with powerful and significant action. Significant action is not about revitalization; it is about reinvention—creating something new.

The track record for mastering major transitions is dismal, even when the inaction can kill. Dr. Edward Miller, the dean of the medical school at Johns Hopkins University, reports, "If you look at people after coronary-artery bypass grafting two years later, 90% of them have not changed their lifestyle." Nine out of ten are stuck in a lifestyle that is killing them. And the track record in business is not much better. Most major change efforts fail to fully achieve their objectives. Why is that?

A true transition is an act of moving from one state of being to another. It requires leaving what is familiar and comfortable behind. As the changes in your life mount up, a massive amount of pent-up energy builds and demands to be released. But to be released it must find a gap, an open space to arc across. Like a mounting storm, we feel discontent and dissatisfaction rumbling through our bodies, thundering for release, waiting for the opportunity to strike a new high point. But first we have to pass through an opening, a gap where nothing exists. And that is why transitioning can be so difficult.

To transition we must enter a state in which we are no longer what we once were, and yet we are not who we must become. We have to be willing to stand in the open gap and momentarily risk being nothing. That is why so many retreat to the safety of their past, to the old and familiar. They choose to tolerate the discomfort of their stale complaints instead of risking themselves in the gap.

Transitioning is about courage and facing your greatest fears. This cannot be done with change management techniques alone. It takes heart and commitment, not just technique. It's about challenging the stories you created about yourself that are in conflict with reality. Transitioning is about finding your true voice and discovering the best of who you are. It's putting your gifts, strengths and capabilities to work in a powerful and personally significant way. It not only requires a willingness to be challenged but also acceptance of help and guidance.

Crossing that gap is often done more gracefully and effectively with the support of an experienced guide. That is why I am sharing some of my own transitions as well as those of my clients and other loved ones. These transitions are not being shared because they are more challenging or compelling than your own, but because of the lessons they have taught me. It is my hope that as you read this book, it is not read as a brief autobiography, but rather as a guide for you to look deeply into your own transitions and create your own lessons for your next transition. To help you do that, each chapter will end with a thought to consider or a positive step to take.

And like me, I hope you also discover that it is not the fear of death that moves you, but rather the joy of being vibrantly alive. That is the ultimate calling.

CHAPTER ONE

*In which we learn that transitions are powered by purpose.
Without purpose, your life becomes a dreary journey
without a destination.*

TRANSITIONING INTO PURPOSE

The year was 2000 and I thought I knew where I was headed. It seemed clear enough. I thought I was living my life as a successful corporate executive, about to interview for an exciting new position back east.

I can see now that this life only looked successful on the outside. On the inside I was lost, refusing to face realty. I didn't understand it at the time, but I had been resisting my own transition for years.

I had just resigned as the president of a company I had helped bring from start-up to major worldwide prominence. I thought my resignation was based on boredom. I thought the job just wasn't exciting to me any more. So I decided to look for something new. Something that would excite me more.

I'd had conversations with headhunters and with other companies that were looking for CEOs. At the time I really believed that my next job would be as a CEO. It seemed right. I could take the lessons that I had learned for the last 30 years and share them as a mentor and leader.

At least that was my story as I waited to board the plane to New York. And it was a good story. But it just wasn't true.

At that time, the technology distribution industry was undergoing a massive restructuring. Our company was struggling and so was I. Was I bored? Exhausted? No, the truth was that the thought of failing scared me. But I fought that reality. I denied it. I had my boredom story, a great resume and a burning desire for redemption and another chance.

This trip would be the culmination of many interviews I had done with a number of companies, from very small, venture-funded start-up companies to major European firms (the internet glow was still there—this was the beginning of 2000—venture capital was still flowing). This particular company I was about to do my final interview with was run by a 29-year-old genius inventor who had just received a venture infusion. He was one of these prodigies who had been working since he was 14 years old and had created a number of wireless inventions. He sold his first invention to a local airport when he was 15! He was very dynamic and likable. He had a great team, and was energized by the possibility of creating a great company. I was feeling the old excitement again. The young owner saw me as a mentor and as someone who had made enough mistakes to steer him clear of them. This trip to New York was for me to meet with his board.

I was flying out of Phoenix and, as sometimes happens when there's bad weather in the east, we were on ground delay. The storms at Kennedy Airport would not let up, so we were stuck there for about five hours. After I had read every magazine that I could get my hands on, called all the people that I knew, and checked all my voice mail, I finally couldn't avoid it any longer—I went to my procrastination file. That's where I save torn-out business articles that I know I should read but don't. I just stuff them in a folder and put them in my briefcase.

So I started to tackle that file. And as I was reading through these articles I finally got to the one that was literally the last one in the file. It was dated 1998. It was a little article from *Fast Company* by Richard Leider. He had written a book called *The Power of Purpose*, and he was now talking about the book in an interview in the magazine. A regular contributor to *Fast Company*, Leider had been in the outplacement business working with key executives for 20 years. In writing his book, he had interviewed many of his ex-clients or executives who had retired—all people he knew to be very successful. He asked these people how they were viewing life right now, and what constitutes "the good life."

Leider noticed that invariably, the "good life" answers came back in the form of these three conditions: 1) You are living in a place where you feel you belong, 2) You're in strong and loving relationships at home, at work and with yourself, and 3) You are doing a work that you were truly meant to do in an environment where you fit and are contributing to something you believe in. Finally, they said, you are doing all three of those things with intent and *purpose*.

I can remember reading that article and being struck by that simple truth. I caught a glimpse of my own transition unfolding that day, and my stories started to dissolve.

I sat there suddenly realizing there was *nothing* in my career that I had ever really done with intent and purpose. My career successes had had a lot to do with being lucky—being in the right place at the right time. Events happened, and I took advantage of them. Like a leaf in a stream, I had been swept into a company that was to grow from a fledgling $5 million company to a $7 billion Fortune 500 company and the world's sixth largest technology distributor. I was the president of that distribution business. And even though those years of experience were very satisfying and rewarding, it was nothing I had set out to do on purpose.

I realized for the first time in my life that I had no purpose in mind for myself. I never did. I can remember right then sitting in that airport and thinking about where I was about to fly. What was my purpose there? I didn't know a thing about wireless. I didn't want to live in Boston or New York or anywhere else other than Arizona. This trip was much more dictated by *their* needs than by mine. And I had no idea what I really wanted to do. What was I doing in this airport, then?

As far as I could figure it out, what I was doing had something to do with fulfilling an ego need. I didn't define it in those terms back then, but I was pretty aware that what I was chasing didn't have anything to do with what my true life was about. Or *could be* about if I discovered what I was meant to do. So I made a decision on the spot. I called the chairman of this little company and said, "I'm not coming."

After I explained to him why I wasn't coming, he reminded me that I had promised to be there for the interview. He said he had people flying in from all over to meet with me. And he was right. I didn't want to start my new life by breaking promises, so I decided to meet with the board and tell them about my awakening in the airport.

It wasn't easy. As I sat in the conference room facing all of them, I told them about the article I had read and the impact it had on me. They were very gracious and tried to convince me that they could make it work for me. I told them I was sorry, but I would not ignore the message I'd received. And in that moment, I felt freer than I had in 30 years. (Transitioning does that.)

After that meeting I got back on an airplane and flew back to Phoenix. There was a lot of time to reflect about what had happened over the last 24 hours. I had been blind to all the signals that were telling me it was time to move on and begin a new adventure—to make my next-life transition. Boredom was the first indicator that I was not being personally accountable for my life. It wasn't the job that was boring me. I was boring myself.

When I returned home, my wife Patsy was waiting for me. I told her what had happened and showed her the article. I didn't know what she would think about all this but then I saw that she had started to cry.

"What's wrong?" I said.

"I didn't really want to leave," she said. "This is where we belong."

And I realized she was crying for happiness. We talked more about the article, and living a life on purpose and she asked me, "What do you think you were meant to do?"

"I have no idea."

I took three months off to see if I could find out. I spent most of that time with Patsy, traveling together and just being together. I did a lot of reflection and explored some other opportunities that were in Arizona, and it soon dawned on me that 1) I never wanted to retire, and 2) What I most loved doing was working with and mentoring people. Helping them succeed.

So I started to think about being a business advisor and coach as a full-time occupation. I wasn't totally convinced yet, because I didn't really know how being a consultant would work for me. But the more I talked to the people who knew me best, the more they reassured me that it would be a perfect fit. Some went further and affirmed that being an advisor and mentor was exactly what I was meant to do at this stage of my life.

Even though I knew inside that they were right, it took a while for me to trust it. So many people that I ran into who were former executives were wandering around with business cards that said "consultant and coach" on them. The standard response to that was, "How long are you going to be a consultant? Till you get a job?" My commitment would have to run much deeper than that.

I knew from the time I made the decision at the airport that this transition would be a true test of my commitment. But I was surprised by the emotional intensity that came with this transition. It didn't take long before I realized how attached I had become to my corporate identity. Who would I be without the title, corner office, big salary and stock options? It doesn't take long to discover what you most fear when you're at the precipice of a major life transition.

Beyond my own ego issues, I also had to confront practical matters like making money. Making this transition could mean going a long time without any real source of income. Patsy and I decided to sell the house and the luxury cars. We rented a 900-square-foot guesthouse from a friend. It was in that little house that Patsy and I discovered that we were more committed to our future than to the trappings of the past.

We knew we were on the right path, and we didn't waver. After a great deal of reflection, I created my own coaching practice, one that would not be dependent on long-term engagements or interim management projects. I created a practice that would allow me to do the things I most loved…work with people who are fully engaged and not satisfied with the status quo; people who know that they have not reached their pinnacle, who have more to give, more to accomplish, more to express with their life.

It all sounded good, but I had no real idea how to pull it off. The thought of calling a CEO and asking, "Do you have more to achieve?" paralyzed me. Besides, that would be a pretty ineffective way to start. So as a means of introducing myself, I decided to do pro bono speeches for CEO forums, associations and the like.

I met my first client at a business network dinner. He had spent about ten years in the venture capital business helping finance software companies. His dream was to start his own company. When he learned about my background he asked me if I would help him. Soon I had more coaching clients, almost all coming from referrals, and the career I was meant to pursue had begun. For the first time in my life, I was living on purpose. It was a powerful transition up from directionless approval seeking, and it woke me up to the power that transitions could have for others.

Discover Your Purpose

Are you living with purpose? Don't look for someone to tell you. You are the ultimate authority. Your first clue is the amount of positive energy and joy you experience each day. Are you excited when you first wake up? How much of the day is used in activities that you like doing? Are you living your life in accordance with your most deeply held values? Are you making a difference and adding value to something that is important to you and others?

If not a wholehearted "Yes!" to those questions, then the first place to look is within yourself. Before beginning a transition, it is vital to know what moves you and what your core values are.

Write a few pages describing your peak experiences and most vivid memories during your preschool years, grade school, junior high, high school and early adulthood. What beliefs and values emerged from those experiences? Which ones continue to guide and empower you today? Are you expressing those values in your life and work now?

During those peak experiences, what was the source of your motivation—the need for security; the need to love and be loved; for control; for achievement; or to make a difference? What is driving you now and how does that affect the decisions you are making about your life today?

Chapter Two

In which we learn how awareness and acceptance
open you up to accelerated personal growth.

Transition Starts with Reflection

To help clients understand the nature of transition coaching I tell a story to get us started. It's a true story that happened about five years ago. At that time I was 20 pounds heavier than I am right now. Like many men I would look in the mirror and I would say to myself, "You know, for a guy your age, you don't look too bad." I would suck it in a little bit and pull up the belt and tell myself, "For a guy in his 50s you are doing OK!"

Then one day I got out of the shower and was shaving in front of the bathroom mirror. I noticed for the first time that I never let my gaze drop below my chin. I got really curious about that and was suddenly struck with the thought that I was actually avoiding looking at my body. I was afraid to look because of what I would see. Well, I can remember, it was almost like "peeking." I took a quick look down, then another, and finally saw what I had done to myself. That was my first jolt of awareness.

So, I was aware that I weighed much more than I wanted to, but nothing was going to happen unless I was willing to *own* it. By owning it, I mean truly caring about it. Letting my health and my overweight body matter enough for me to do something. And because I wanted to symbolically own it, too, I asked my wife Patsy to come into the bathroom and take pictures of me. And she agreed to take the shots—me standing straight forward and looking at her, me standing sidewise and me with the backside showing: Three pictures of me, bare naked, in all my natural glory. (We didn't have a digital camera then, so I'm sure the guys in the photo lab had a good laugh.)

Although Patsy agreed to take the pictures, she was horrified. She thought I was absolutely nuts. And so did I after we got the pictures back. I looked at them, and it was painful, because it was far worse than what I was seeing through the filter of my own denial, even when I thought I was being "brutally aware." People say a picture is worth a thousand words, but these pictures were worth more than that. Transitioning can't happen until the truth is welcomed into consciousness.

My next act of ownership was to put those pictures in a prominent place where I could see them. Of course, we would take them down when company came over, but I had them near the refrigerator and other places where I could see my current reality. It wasn't long before these constant, painful visual reality-checks did their intended job. It helped me get in touch with my core values, and I committed to do something about it. I took action. The 20 pounds came off, and my transition held. I've never gained the pounds back and I've never looked back.

When I tell my new client this story, it becomes clear that I am here to be that mirror for him. Maybe he is just "peeking" or afraid to look at what's real in his life. My role is to show him that reality is friendly, and can inspire him and can work with him to get virtually anything he wants. But that transition won't happen without his looking in a mirror and reflecting on where he is right now.

My being fat wasn't a "bad" thing once I decided to use it to get what I really wanted. I was beginning to understand something profound: reality always wants to help. And a true transition depends on first accepting reality for what it is.

Get a Daily Dose of Reality

There are two very simple ways to get started, one is an internal inquiry and the other is external. For an external vantage, ask three to five people who know you well these questions about one of your significant responsibilities—manager, member, or mentor, for example:

- *What am I doing extremely well that you would recommend that I keep doing?*
- *What should I start doing that I am not already doing now?*
- *What should I stop doing that would improve my effectiveness?*

When it comes to your personal life, what do you truly care about— your health, personal relationships, financial freedom, home, fun and recreation, spirituality, personal growth and learning, career, or community? Identify what really matters and then assess your level of satisfaction for your current level of performance in each area on a scale from one to ten, with one being the lowest level of satisfaction. Choose one area to improve during the next 90 days by at least one or two points, from a 3 to a 5, for example.

CHAPTER THREE

In which we learn how a powerful intention can trump the fear of failure.

INVESTING IN YOUR TRANSITION

As in every other business I've owned or led, I invested in my coaching practice. Over the last several years, I've earned 72 hours of postgraduate credits for coaching certifications. I read voraciously, continuously adding to my professional skills. I was certified to administer a number of psychometric assessments. I engaged two Ph.Ds to teach me the science of leadership assessment and executive selection. I hired my own coach, Steve Hardison, a man renowned for his transformational work. I served as an adjunct consultant at one of the nation's largest outplacement firms, coaching senior executives in career transition. Not only was I helping other people transition in their own careers, but I was also helping myself do the same thing!

I've learned as I helped those other executives transition that they were often unable to connect with the much-overused advice to "find their passion." For most of the people I've coached and for myself, "passion" implied a certain intimacy that is reserved for a very special loved one. They weren't interested in discovering their passion, but instead were deeply committed to learning what engaged and energized them. Therefore it helped me to think instead about *what I loved doing* rather than what I was "passionate" about. Perhaps it's just semantics, but personally I find that I am energized by thoughts of what I love to do.

After several years of consulting and coaching, I knew and *could say* exactly what I loved to do. So I wrote it down. Try this yourself and write straight from the heart what you love to do. You just might find that there is a transition waiting for you.

I have to admit that early on I found it difficult to trust what was in my heart. It felt too soft. I had disciplined myself for years to think and judge, not feel. Yet I found the words from my heart were far more compelling than what my logic dictated. Once I reached what was in my heart, the words flowed without much thought or effort. When I read it back to myself, I was surprised. I didn't know those words were in me. I realized this was the work I was meant to do. I knew that this is what I wanted to do for the rest of my life. Here's what I wrote:

"I love to inspire, freeing people from the shackles of self-limiting beliefs and self-defeating behavior. I love being a fire-starter, someone who ignites possibility and personal power in others. I love the intimacy and the spiritual bond I create with an engaged and committed client. I love being a cause for personal discovery and growth. I love the exultation of personal triumph. I love working with the whole person—mind, body and spirit. I love being a witness to my clients' discovery of their gifts and talents. I love their courage as they not only face their weaknesses and lies about their limitations, but also face the truth about their innate greatness and unlimited possibilities. I respect what it takes…I face my own each day!"

Facing my own self-limiting beliefs has been an unexpected gift from my coaching practice. Every challenge a client takes on has taught me something about myself. My coaching is not about telling people where they've gone wrong. It's far more effective to simply share where I've derailed myself. My work is to help clients discover and trust their own wisdom.

From those tentative moments with Patsy, unable to say what I loved to do, I had come a long way toward crystallizing my intent. The more I invested in my practice, the more I received from it. The more I practiced, the more I learned. The more I learned, the more I served. And I loved it.

Using Intention to Get Unstuck

If you are feeling stuck, it could be a signal that you have not done the work to identify your ideal future (what you would love doing) or that you have not properly prepared for it. Both identifying your ideal future and preparing for it requires an investment of your time, energy and resources. A great place to start is with Steve Chandler's book Reinventing Yourself. *Once you've created your life vision, then read Frederick Hudson's book* The Adult Years—Mastering the Art of Self-Renewal *and James Loehr's* The Power of Full Engagement *for additional guidance.*

CHAPTER FOUR

In which we learn how to use collaboration to ensure our best effort and highest level of accountability

PEOPLE CAN HELP YOU TRANSITION

Successful transitioning to the next level of life can happen much faster with a coach who will hold you accountable. Coaches are often the most reliable route to an immediate reality-check.

My airport awakening was a full jolt of reality delivered in the form of a business article about living on purpose. My weight loss also occurred because I accepted new reality and altered my thinking accordingly.

This is why I like to tell my new coaching clients the shaving mirror story. It is a gentle opening to the entire concept of transitioning to the life you really want, with reality serving you every step of the way.

My decision to go into coaching was also influenced by the benefits that I myself had received from coaches over the years. Coaching has often given me that wake-up-to-reality "rap" across the brow that the Zen masters liked to do with their students. In Zen training, the masters often used a branch or switch. And I've experienced that metaphysical "Zen rap" more than once from good coaches.

My first coach was an instructor who taught me in the fundamentals of a martial art known as Progressive Fighting Systems. In the training we used rattan sticks 18" to 24" long to simulate weapons. These sticks caused an intense stinging sensation when you were struck by them, but they weren't heavy enough to do any real damage. I'd be going through my choreographed energy moves (taken from the Filipino martial arts) and if my instructor saw me losing attention, I would get a rap. He would strike, stab or slice me with the stick, showing me exactly what would happen if my opponent had been using a real weapon.

I now knew that coaching could be like that. A good coach can spot those unreal, untruthful moments and "move in," usually in the form of a question or observation that interrupts the client's negative pattern of thought.

An executive coach I had once "rapped" me in just that way. There had been an awkward moment of implied criticism of me in a senior management team meeting. At the lunch break, I left the conference room and ate alone in my office. A little while later my coach found me and said, "Jim, you really seem to have been hurt by that." I was taken aback by my coach's observation. Hurt? Real men don't get hurt. They get angry! So I reacted defensively.

"Hurt?" I said. "Hell, I wasn't hurt. I was mad, and I still am mad!"

He looked at me for a while and then he said, "Hurt is often what's at the core of our anger. So if I had to guess, I'd say the way you were questioned in that meeting hurt your feelings, and you left hurt and embarrassed."

Ouch. I'd just felt the rap. But once the sting subsided, the rap served its purpose and focused my attention on a new reality. It increased my awareness of how my thoughts affect my emotional response to the world, no matter how quickly I try to cover hurt feelings with macho anger.

Moments like these power the first stage—the discovery stage—of the coaching journey toward transition. Let's discover what's real. At the beginning, what's real isn't always easy to accept. That's why agreeing to be coached is such an act of courage. In *Good to Great* by Jim Collins, "The Stockdale Paradox" offers a wonderful parallel to coaching when it quotes Admiral Stockdale who said of his prisoner of war experience, "Never lose faith that you will prevail, and at the same time confront the most brutal facts of your current reality."

The martial arts I studied offered another useful foundation for coaching. (Now don't get the wrong impression. I'm not really a fighter. I would rather hug a person than hit him. But I did enjoy learning the art, especially the art of street fighting as taught by the legendary Paul Vunak.) From the very first day of street fighting training I was taught to take in and perceive more than the immediate threat. Not only did I learn to size up my opponents, but I also learned to assess the total reality of the environment.

This is no time for self-deception. I took in and evaluated the full surroundings. What objects might be used as weapons? Are there other people near? What's the ground surface like? Is it ground, floor, concrete, dirt or grass? Each surface presented hidden opportunities and challenges. Finally, I was taught to use many different arts at once: boxing, kickboxing, wrestling, trapping and finishing with head butts, elbows and knees.

This total-reality, maximum-opportunity training gave me a great metaphor for coaching clients into their next transition. This is not a time for self-deception, either. Most clients have no idea whatsoever how many opportunities they have before them. Or how many talents they have at their disposal. Coaching shines a light on all of those exciting elements.

If you are my client, it's your agenda. It's your future we are working on together. Day by day, week by week. And if you are a human being you will resist change! You will even go unconscious to reality. And my job is to then help you see the rest of the picture below your face in the mirror. And to help you alter your thinking so that reality no longer scares you. It now becomes your friend.

Without a coach, or some form of mentor with a mirror, people tend to repeat past mistakes. Past experiences dictate their future. But with coaching they soon realize that being influenced by the past is just a choice. The past is *not* some irresistible force driving their present reality. Breakthroughs begin when the past is challenged.

If you are working with me, challenge is a part of the process. And only because you have much more potential and possibility in you than you can see yourself.

Most of us are aware that the margin of victory is slim—one or two baskets, strokes, hits, strides or seconds. It's what separates champions from the rest of the pack. It is the difference between outstanding and average. Yet we seldom seek the marginal difference for ourselves.

If you've ever lifted weights or done an exercise that requires repetition like sit-ups, you probably started with a goal in mind—10, 20, 50 or maybe 100 reps. Most people either fall short or reach the goal and stop. After a while, they begin to plateau and progress levels off. It's like hitting a wall.

Having a partner or a coach ask for "one more rep" can change all that forever. Because your imagined barrier comes tumbling down, and you realize it was all in your mind. Your coach's story about you has more power in it than your own. It shatters your old story and a whole new possibility opens up for personal growth.

My clients are usually surprised to learn that what separates them from transitioning to their next level of success are merely imagined barriers. I'm not talking about breaking the laws of physics or balancing a Buick on the end of your little finger. I am saying that what separates you from what you want in your life and career is only a thought.

In the discovery phase of coaching, I am listening for those thoughts that either generate power for my client or limits her. Through inquiry we will challenge those beliefs that limit action. We will investigate the thoughts that narrow the client's perspective of what is possible.

I also know that we are all very different people. As Deepak Chopra says, "We have all walked in different gardens and knelt at different graves." So a transition that is simple for one client may be terrifying for another. Self-limiting beliefs can bloom into full-blown phobias over time. So my challenge for you to clear your particular hurdle is delivered as an invitation, not an expectation.

Discover the Power of Collaboration

If you are like me, you can probably easily identify an important practice in your life in which you haven't been performing at your highest possible level or even an adequate level. You may even be backsliding after making a little progress. If there is something you want to improve, find a friend to be your accountability partner. Here's how it works:

- *Each partner starts by establishing a specific and measurable goal with a beginning and ending date.*
- *Set yourself up to succeed. You probably have already mastered failure. Let's focus on success. During the first week, make it easy and enjoyable by identifying one small thing you could do to move toward your goal. For example, if you are focused on fitness but haven't exercised for several years, start out by promising to walk 15 minutes on at least 3 days during the next week, for example. Don't start out by promising to run 3 miles every day. Remember this is a commitment, a promise to perform, and must not be broken under any circumstance.*
- *Put it in writing: "I, Jim, promise to walk for at least 15 minutes on Monday, Thursday and Saturday." Sign your name under your written promise, date it and give it to your partner.*
- *Track and record your progress. Report the results to your partner each week.*
- *Create a beneficial and supportive reward for success. It doesn't have to be a big deal, just something you enjoy. Take your daughter out for a small ice cream cone, for example.*
- *Raise the bar each week by increasing the frequency and/or the duration of the selected practice. Continue to error on the side of setting yourself up to succeed, not easily, but with a focused and determined effort.*

CHAPTER FIVE

In which we learn that courage is not a character trait but rather a conscious decision.

TRANSITIONS CAN REDEFINE COURAGE

Accepting feedback as an invitation has changed my life more than once. One day, almost 15 years ago, I was sitting in a restaurant having lunch with a friend and business mentor when he looked at me and said, "Jim, do you know you didn't smile at that waiter?"

And I said, "Yeah, so?"

My friend said, "You didn't even look at him."

"He got my order, didn't he?"

"Jim, there's another human being standing in front of you, being nice to you and you didn't even acknowledge that. What's the matter with you?"

I was surprised by what he was saying to me. It was one of those "rap" moments where I felt the sting of the master's stick. I realized right then and there that I was treating that waiter the same way I was treating my business associates and maybe even my family. I was so wrapped up in my own worries that other people might as well have been robots, like the waiter who had taken my order.

My friend and I started talking about my dismissive way with people when he asked me a question no one had ever asked me before. He said, "Jim, have you ever considered therapy?"

"What do you mean?"

"You just seem so angry. You seem like you are not in a particularly good place."

Then he shared with me some therapeutic work he himself had done and how he had begun reading Joseph Campbell. He said, "I found in Campbell's study of mythology great messages of hope. They offered me a whole new perspective on life."

So I signed up for 10 sessions with a therapist and also started reading Joseph Campbell. I found it to be a wonderful, healing experience. The therapy was my first real complete conversation about the things I had never talked to anybody else about—fears, self-esteem, judgments, and my experiences in Vietnam.

I also started benefiting from reading Joseph Campbell. Campbell was convinced, through his study of ancient mythology, that anyone's life could become a hero's journey—a passionate pursuit of something you really care about. Campbell's famous prescription for finding your path was to "follow your bliss" and not let fear stop you. To return home and find the true self, the hero always had to first face his greatest fear.

I was really taken by Campbell's accounts of the mythological journeys of the hero. I didn't know at the time that his writing was calling to that part of me that would later want to partner with people in facilitating their own heroic transitional journeys out of the darkness of self-limitation to full expression of their potential. That is the ultimate transition waiting for all of us.

At that time, more than 20 years ago, it was also connecting with a different yearning inside me—something I didn't fully understand. All my life it had seemed that there was always something calling me to be more than I was. For example, I had always been attracted to heroes. I'd grown up in the '50s and '60s when westerns were prominent in the popular culture. I was spellbound by western myths and heroes: John Wayne…Alan Ladd in the movie *Shane*…Steve McQueen in *The Great Escape*, and all those wonderful courageous characters.

In my ten sessions of therapy, I felt part of my journey moving forward. I learned that the things that were limiting me—recklessness, irresponsible behavior or seeking danger—were not genetic. I didn't have to be like my father—a World War II Army Air Corps officer and my earliest hero—who had been sometimes an angry, wayward and daring youth. Once I could recognize my own nonsense and process it, and forgive it, I was better able to understand and accept the personal challenge of others. Transitioning is at first an inside job, a process of looking inward and finding the truth about yourself.

Through reading Joseph Campbell I realized that my yearning was not unique. Many people, from all cultures and from all periods of recorded history, experience the same yearning, the same desire to know their strengths and use them fully, and to find their purpose and make a contribution. Or, as George Bernard Shaw said, "This is the true joy in life, to be used for a purpose recognized by yourself as a mighty one."

I thought I had been burned out and bored by my external circumstance in corporate America, but I can now see that I was suffering more from an internal lack of vision. As the poet David Whyte has said, the cure for exhaustion is not rest. It is wholeheartedness! As my "successful" life as a business executive was proving, my own exhaustion was caused by living my life through an identity created to fulfill the expectation of others.

This driven but "successful" identity I'd worked feverishly to create was an attempt to win approval by demonstrating courage and strength. A striving to be more than I was. A transition waiting to happen.

I had tested myself like this before. After my sophomore year in college, I was drafted by the U.S. Army. I could have joined another branch of the service like the Navy or the Air Force, but I joined the infantry so I could experience action in Vietnam. I needed to prove something. I was looking for validation.

This had been a lifelong quest. Early on, even in childhood, I started to listen and look for what was missing—in me and in the world. My fight with reality had started at an early age.

In a bizarre way, this behavior seemed to serve me. I could find what's missing and fulfill it! I could be the one who sees what's wrong and makes it the way things should be. I developed a keen eye for imperfection. I could spot it a mile away. Even better, I could see ways to improve it and then fix it. That particular habit of mine, seeing imperfection, became my source of success…and my greatest limitation.

The love, the rewards and the recognition I received for constantly challenging and improving the status quo were addictive. I was never satisfied. I couldn't get enough of it to ever feel fulfilled. How could I? Nothing could ever be good enough, including me. It was only a thought, but it was powerful enough to create how I experienced the world.

But even up to very recently I was struggling with thoughts of whether something was still missing—some element of courage— or maybe courage itself. When I first met my current coach, Steve Hardison—an extraordinary, challenging charismatic man—I could see that if I agreed to work with him he wouldn't let me off the hook. I knew that I would have to face what I had been avoiding for decades. I told him, "I don't know if I have the courage to work with you."

Immediately he stopped me short and explained that courage is not something anybody has. It's not like brown eyes or blue eyes— it's not a characteristic. It is merely a creation—a thought. It can be created by anyone. Or not. And what would be at play here would not be whether I had the courage to work with him. It would be whether I would create the courage to work on *myself.*

In that unforgettable moment with Steve Hardison I understood courage in a new way. I could suddenly see that courage was an always-available choice for action. And that I could generate any action I wanted if I could understand and change my thoughts.

Understanding the Power of Your Thoughts

The most important concept I have ever learned is that every emotion I experience is the effect of my own thinking, and that for each and every one of my thoughts I have a choice—to believe it or not. Accepting this has been the basis for the most profound changes in my life.

I have learned that nothing makes me happy or sad, angry or peaceful, fearful or courageous, loving or hateful other than what I think. Nothing can have a lasting emotional effect on me unless I choose to let it. Will I react to what you, they or it does? Probably, and that's usually a good thing, but making it a lasting effect is my choice. As my friend, Chris Dorris, a performance psychologist and mental toughness trainer, points out, this is not positive thinking. It is disciplined thinking, and it can make a profound difference in your life as well.

CHAPTER SIX

In which we learn that challenging experiences can be the source of great wisdom, but only if we stop deceiving ourselves about what really happened.

A SPIRIT BEYOND "MANHOOD"

When I wondered whether I "had" the courage inside me to work with such a powerful and demanding coach, he was able to show me right there that my focus was on winning or losing the approval of someone outside of me, and that the true joy or "courage" of life was an inside game.

Whatever it is that we do in the face of difficulty (that we later call courage) is a created act. It's a creation of doing what needs to be done in that moment. It's not drawing upon some genetic well of courage. And it never occurred to me as being a creation before this conversation.

Immediately I wanted to tell Steve about an experience I had in Vietnam—something I hadn't spoken to anyone about before. I'd always had a hard time making sense of it, but I thought maybe now I could.

It was 1967 and I was a wild, shaggy-haired youth just recently kicked out of college, living in a cabin in Keystone, South Dakota, having the time of my life working with friends on a tramway for tourists and partying every weekend.

I thought it just didn't get much better than that! I was up there working hard and having fun with no parents, no college and total freedom, when I looked down the hill one day and saw my dad's yellow Cadillac making its way up the road to the tourist center.

What's this? I had probably seen my Dad once or twice since I had been kicked out of college, which seemed fine for both me and him, so why was this retired Air Force colonel pulling into the tramway parking lot while I was up on the deck loading passengers into the tram? I looked down to see my Dad coming up the stairs to the deck where I was working and he had a look on his face that I used to dread. I called it the "Colonel Look." I knew this wasn't going to be a good meeting.

He walked up to me and he said, "Son, do you have a minute— I'd like to talk to you."

I said, "What's up, Dad?"

He looked at my long hair and said, "Who is your barber?"

"I don't have a barber."

And he reached in his pocket and pulled out an envelope and handed it to me saying, "You do now."

I opened the envelope while my father, the former colonel, stood there watching me and saw that it was my military draft notice. I had just been drafted.

"Son," he said, "whatever you do, get in the Navy, join the Air Force—don't go into the Army."

Because my dad had been in WWII, he knew that going into the army in this Vietnam era was the most dangerous route one could take.

So, of course, I chose to ignore his advice and went straight into the Army. I'd show the world who had courage. I'd go right into the infantry if I could, so I could see combat action.

My father knew from his own experiences what being in the infantry meant, especially in Vietnam. But for me being in the infantry was, again, a heroic call. To me being in the infantry would be like watching a Rambo movie. I didn't want to do my time someplace typing letters.

After basic training, I was sent to Fort Polk in Louisiana for advance infantry training. On January 1, 1968, I was on my way to Vietnam and 30 days later the Tet offensive began. More than 70,000 North Vietnam soldiers and an untold number of Vietcong guerilla fighters surged into at least 100 towns and cities, including Saigon. My unit, the 199th Light Infantry Brigade, would be in the thick of that fight.

After four months of combat and continuing skirmishes, I was wounded for the second time, seriously enough to be sent home. But something else happened that day that would affect me much more than the wounds. Several companies from the 199th were converging on an area where we knew a North Vietnamese Army regiment had been operating. We had to hack our way with machetes through thick jungle to approach the area. As we broke through to a clearing, we suddenly realized that we had stumbled right into the middle of the enemy base camp. By the time my company arrived the North Vietnamese had retreated across the clearing into some denser areas of the jungle. We were moving in on them and taking a lot of fire. I was the acting squad leader.

Along with a couple of new guys who had only been in country for several weeks, we also had a new lieutenant because our former lieutenant, whom I had admired so much, had been killed about two weeks before. Because of the inexperienced people in my squad, I decided to take the point that day—moving out in front of my squad about 10 yards. So there we were with a new lieutenant and a number of rookies, slowly advancing into the jungle.

As I moved deeper into the jungle, I could hear wounded American soldiers right in front of me. I couldn't spot them because I couldn't see more than 10 feet or so in front of me, but I could hear what sounded like a half-dozen wounded men screaming for help. A barrage of heavy rifle and machine gun fire pinned them down. I knew approximately where the other companies were in relationship to me, but somehow these men had gotten in front of me.

It sounded like they were maybe fifty yards in front of me, and then a movement suddenly caught my eye. I looked over to my right and saw another young man a few feet away who I took to be an American medic. He appeared to be unarmed and wasn't wearing a helmet—a handsome man with well-groomed, dark black hair. Our eyes met. I'm sure it was less than a second, but it seemed like our eyes were locked together for much longer. And then in a flash, I knew that this was a North Vietnamese enemy soldier. I dropped to the ground immediately, lifted my rifle to shoot but he was gone.

In combat training, it had been drilled into me over and over that my job would have been to capture or kill him without hesitation. But something strange had momentarily come over me. Even though I knew I was walking into enemy lines, the minute I looked into this man's eyes I saw him as a friend.

It was a disturbing flash that went against all my training and desire to be a hero. I questioned myself long after it happened. Yet somehow I think I can see now that something important had shown itself. In that moment that I looked in his eyes there was a recognition. What was it? Universal love and connection? Whatever it was it was real, and it was closer to the true, deep spirit that I carried with me than anything I'd experienced before. In that moment in the jungle, the real spirit in me had seen itself. Would I be able to handle—or even understand—the transition that was calling to me?

A Call to Discover Your True Spirit

What was your most emotionally charged moment? Please take a moment and recall it. What happened and how did you react— with fear, anger, or grief? Since that incident, how have you judged yourself and the other people involved?

Make a few notes and then read on. Further guidance for this discovery will be provided in the next chapter.

CHAPTER SEVEN

In which we learn to find peace through the power of forgiveness.

ENDING YOUR OWN WAR

As I was lying there on the ground and looking at where that North Vietnamese soldier had darted back into the jungle, I saw the branches moving, so I quickly aimed for where he had run. But again I didn't shoot because that was directly where I was hearing those wounded soldiers. Within a second or two, I myself started taking fire.

I was in a small open area, surrounded by jungle plants and high trees. Whoever had those wounded GIs pinned down had a new target—me. I couldn't see them, but gunfire was coming from the trees somewhere in front of me. First from the right, then from the left and then from both sides simultaneously. At least two snipers had me in their rifle sights.

During those first few moments, my best friend, Al, and another soldier had managed to crawl within 25 feet of me, just off to my right behind a tree. As I looked over at them, I saw the ground around us erupting in a burst of machine gun fire. One of the rounds smashed into my right elbow, tearing several inches of bone and flesh out of my upper arm. It felt like I had been hit with a sledgehammer—like someone had taken a 10-pound sledge-hammer and slammed it into my elbow. I could feel my whole arm being crushed into the ground.

The impact was so great that it literally knocked me senseless. I stopped thinking, feeling, hearing or seeing. Everything went black for a second. As my head cleared, I realized I couldn't feel my arm. There was no sensation from the middle of my upper arm all the way down to my fingers. I felt nothing there. I was convinced that my arm had been severed by the gunshot.

Still stunned, I could feel bullets ripping into the ground underneath my legs. The snipers were now aiming for my thighs, but the shots were missing. In Vietnam, it was a common guerrilla tactic to wound U.S. troops badly enough to immobilize them without killing them. That would draw in two or three more soldiers attempting a rescue but making them all targets for a kill.

Even in that dazed state, I knew that I had to get up and scramble over to Al where there was more cover, but I had a problem. I couldn't figure out how to hold my rifle and get up without my right arm dropping out of my sleeve. I laid there confused and groggy, playing dead and trying to gather myself.

Seeing that I had been hit and wasn't moving, Al started yelling for a medic. Through clenched teeth, I was trying to tell him to shut up! I knew we'd all be killed if they tried to pull me out.

Suddenly there was a break in the fire. I rolled over on my back, pulled my right arm against my chest, and somehow got to my knees and on my feet. I stumbled the 25 feet over to Al. He put a field dressing on the wound and half carried, half dragged me a couple hundred yards to a clearing where the wounded were being evacuated by helicopter.

Lying there among the wounded, I let what had just happened sink in. I had been in dozens of firefights before and had fired hundreds of rounds at distant Vietcong and NVA soldiers. But when I was face to face with the enemy, I didn't pull the trigger. And when wounded, I stopped fighting.

I began to question myself right then and there as I waited for the chopper to come in. Did I make the right decision by not firing? Who lived and who died as a result of my action? Was I a coward? I created negative stories around those questions and then let the answers haunt me for years.

Even though I can now see that the split second in the jungle had shown me my true nature, my belief system wouldn't let that truth in. But as William Blake once said, "a fool who persists in his folly will become wise." I would later see that recycling the past would never allow me to transition. Transitioning can only find traction in the present moment.

This insight, gained years later, about the difference between reality and my negative, limited thought patterns, would become the core element in my coaching of others. Reality is almost never what we think.

In the previous chapter we had the opportunity to learn that our most challenging experiences can be the source of great wisdom, but only if we stop deceiving ourselves about what really happened. What was your most emotionally charged moment? What happened and how did you react—with fear, anger, or grief? Write your story and express your deepest thoughts and feelings about your experience.

After you've written it, put it aside for a while and take a break. When you come back, reread what you've written and highlight all the interpretations, judgments and evaluations you've assigned to the event, to yourself and the others involved. How would your story read if all those interpretations were deleted?

The event I experienced in Vietnam would read as follows: A man walked in the jungle. He heard other men asking for help. He saw another man and dropped to the ground. He was shot in the arm. He got up and another man helped him.

That is what happened, but that was not what caused the pain. It was my own interpretation and judgment about the event that hurt. And those judgments were so severe that I believed I deserved to be unrelentingly punished. I did that for more than thirty years.

It wasn't until I learned to forgive myself that I was released from the prison in which I locked myself for decades. Who else could truly forgive me? My coach, Steve Hardison, once questioned why I was waiting for God to do something I was unwilling to do myself. I was the one doing the judging, not God. It was my job to forgive myself first. I eventually learned that until I forgave myself someone else's forgiveness would be meaningless. And until I learned to forgive myself, I would be unable to forgive others.

Today many American vets are visiting Vietnam and sitting down to have a drink with their former enemies. They discovered a new truth. There is an element of spirit and humanity that people identify with when they are face-to-face with their enemy. The war is over. Not just on the battlefield, but in your mind.

People I coach have their own wars going on. They have struggles with other people. They have battles and they feel wounded by the betrayal of others. My work is to help them transition from this painful emotional battlefield into the world of spirit and joy. My work is also to show them the gifts they have to exchange. The story of Alison will show you what I mean.

A Call for Forgivenes

To forgive doesn't mean to condone or approve. It is an act of pardoning, and to do that one must discover the greater truth. Steve Hardison helped me discover my truth through a simple yet powerful practice. He had me say the words "I am..." and then listen for the internal judgments my mind created. The first one surprised me. It was "I am a liar." I spent one morning discovering my judgments and listed several pages of negative self-concepts.

For each one of those judgments, I wrote "I forgive myself for judging myself as a _____, for the truth is _____." It wasn't easy. It took several weeks to complete the first pass. Then we tested each one. If I hesitated or could not own the truth, we did more work until I could see and own a greater truth than the negative judgment.

The final release occurred after Steve introduced me to a form of inquiry developed by Byron Katie. "Katie," as she is called, is perhaps one of our greatest living teachers for helping people discover their greater truth. If you are still unwilling to forgive yourself or someone else, please visit her web site at www.thework.com where you'll find free resources as well as other references to guide you in the process.

CHAPTER EIGHT

In which we learn that getting someone out of the way isn't the path to success. It's getting out of your own way.

ALISON ASKS FOR COACHING

Alison was the Vice President of Sales & Marketing in a family-owned, fast-growing wooden door manufacturer that had doubled in size during the building boom in the southwest. The daughter of the founder and CEO, she had worked her way up to that post from an entry-level sales position.

Alison was known for her drive and passion for the business. And no one was surprised to learn that Alison had recently gone to her father and demanded to be promoted to President & Chief Operating Officer (COO).

Because it wasn't an unreasonable demand. Most of the company's success could be directly attributed to Alison's ability to recruit, manage and grow their dealer base. The dealers trusted her, and they loved her ability turn their feedback into highly effective marketing programs and product improvements.

But Alison had become frustrated with the company's growth.

She thought that finance and manufacturing were dragging their feet and obstructing almost all her expansive ideas. So she wanted more control.

Her father, Frank, was ready to listen to his daughter's ambitious request. He had always wanted Alison to succeed him. It had been a dream of his since he had first taken his little girl to the office with him on a Saturday morning almost 25 years ago.

Besides, because he was no longer active in the management of the company, Frank was ready to retire soon. So the timing wasn't off. But something else was, and Frank struggled to explain it.

Although he would be happy to have her in that top position, Frank wasn't totally convinced Alison herself was ready to be Chief Operating Officer of the company. She had only been in a leadership position for three years.

But Alison was persistent, and Frank ultimately relented, despite his misgivings. He was still worried about how the other managers would react, especially the operations managers who would soon be reporting to her. That's when Alison called me for help. She knew my work was all about transitioning, and she was on the verge of a major career transition.

At the time, no one other than Alison, her father, and a few outside advisors knew that she was about to be promoted. And all of them were very concerned that Nolan, the company CFO, would resign immediately when he heard the news. Nolan's and Alison's dislike for each other was well known throughout the company. The battle lines in the company had been clearly drawn.

For several years, Nolan believed he'd been getting strong signals from Frank that *he* would be the one promoted to COO. Like many CFOs, Nolan wanted to break out of the accounting role and demonstrate his capability in operations. He not only wanted to show how good he was, he honestly believed he was the only logical choice for the COO position.

And he had a point! When Nolan came to the company, its financial and accounting systems were a complete disaster. The former accounting manager and his staff weren't prepared to deal with the company's growth. Nolan quickly assessed the situation and turned the department around in a matter of months. Impressed by Nolan's effectiveness, Frank gave him responsibility for the IT department where he proved equally competent managing the technology side of the business.

In Frank's management team meetings, Nolan was always well prepared and knew the numbers better than anyone in the company. In fact, no one could remember Nolan ever losing an argument with another manager about financial details, no matter which department or line item was being discussed. Fearing

Nolan's challenging questions and endless suggestions for improvements, most of the managers dreaded the monthly management meeting.

Nolan was logical, factual, and incisive. Proud of his ability to challenge and defeat emotionally or intuitively presented proposals, he had effectively derailed almost every initiative made by Alison and her marketing team.

But, despite his intimidating expertise, Nolan was secretly afraid of Alison.

He often felt uncomfortable with her passion and energy. He thought she could be a loose cannon and even a little dangerous with all her wild ideas. From his point of view, she always wanted to throw money at unproven marketing ideas and new product concepts. He was afraid her passion and energy might overwhelm the company's secure stability.

I spent several hours with Alison in our initial coaching session. I wanted to hear what her thinking was like. The ups and the downs. How did she mentally process her peak moments and most important life experiences? I wanted to understand what energized her as well as what drained her.

Effective coaching reflects the part of the Prayer of St. Francis that asks, "Grant that I not so much seek to be understood as to understand." If I was going to be able to help Alison, I would have to have a very thorough understanding of how she saw the world around her. I would have to know who I was coaching before I would know how to proceed. You can't transition from a place you've never understood.

And as I listened on in that session, I learned some interesting things about Alison and her imaginary rivals.

Know Your Competition

Who is your real competition? Who is making it tough for you to get what you want? Maybe it's an internal rival within your company or maybe it's someone who just sent the CEO a great resume. Or maybe your greatest competitor is no one other than yourself. What ultimately gets in the way of future success could be what you don't know or don't want to know about yourself today.

Many people don't feel understood largely because they're unable to express to others how they think, feel and experience the world. It is a jumble of perceptions and mental concepts filtered by beliefs, stories, motives, values, and attitudes. And yet they feel certain about how things should be or shouldn't be and what is right or wrong with you, them, it or me. They can't say why, they just know. They especially know when they encounter someone who thinks and feels differently than they do. It is their own lack of understanding themselves that is the source of their prejudice about others.

As mentors or coaches, one of our most important obligations is to understand and appreciate our clients without judgment. It is the coach's total appreciation and acceptance that neutralizes the clients' fear of knowing themselves—their strengths, weaknesses, behavior type, values, motives and leadership attributes. Once they start to understand their own mental habits and preferred ways of experiencing the world, their automatic judgments about themselves and others start to soften. When they accept that the only way to change the world is to change themselves, the barriers to success come down.

CHAPTER NINE

In which we learn how holding back the truth and filtering feedback can turn confidence into arrogance.

INTRODUCING: THE TRUTH

During my first session with Alison, I learned what she wanted to accomplish and contribute as the COO. And we talked about what she was worried about and the source of those concerns.

Earlier I had given her an in-depth questionnaire about her values and aspirations, allowing her several days to reflect enough to express herself fully. She had also taken a number of on-line psychometric assessments that provided us a summary of her management style, her leadership attributes, and her core values. We also had a multirater survey (360 degree feedback) underway that would help us understand how her direct reports, peers, and key partners experienced her leadership. These intake assessments (and sometimes more) are standard with me. (Many people see coaching as an undisciplined, gut-level, hit-or-miss process. But, when done properly, coaching is thorough and comprehensive, while still retaining the great capacity for the quantum breakthrough.)

These analyses were allowing Alison to learn about herself. When people have a chance to step back and study their own thinking patterns, a surprising thing happens. They see that they are *not* their thinking patterns. There is so much more to them than the thoughts and beliefs that limit their lives.

It was good to see Alison participate so thoroughly in this process, because I knew it could eventually assist her transition.

Alison had the personal attributes that many people experience as "natural leadership." Outgoing and charming, she easily influenced people with her warmth. She was unrestrained and direct. One never had to guess what was on her mind. There was also a kind of contagious restless energy about her. She loved the fast pace of her business and the variety of challenges she took on. Under pressure, she could be forceful and commanding. She was clearly in charge.

Alison also wanted things fast and simple. She hated getting bogged down with details. Needing only a few facts to make a decision, she tended to leap to the most favorable conclusion—the one she wanted in the first place. Rules were written to serve her and if they didn't, she broke the rules. Her people loved her passion, fearlessness and creativity. They were extremely loyal and looked to her as their mentor and protector.

But Alison, for all her positive attributes, had a major problem.

It went by the name of Nolan.

It wasn't long in our session before Alison had launched into a tirade about the company's CFO. Oh, she grudgingly respected his business acumen and analytical skills. But to her Nolan was mostly a problem.

"Tell me about why he bothers you so," I said.

"He drives me crazy," she said. "His endless questions and constant need for more information. It becomes irrational, and it's a morale-killer. Don't get me wrong; I know I need him here, at least in the near term. I know I have a lot to learn about operations and finance. And he does have the knowledge."

But working with him had become nearly impossible. Because over the last year, their relationship had deteriorated to a new low. Unless they were in a mandatory meeting together, they seldom spoke to each other. Most of their communication was through chilly emails, even though their offices were less than 20 feet apart. When they were face to face, it almost always ended in a bitter debate.

As she went on about all her challenges with Nolan, I began to smile to myself. They were perfect for each other! I could see that they would be useful spiritual teachers for each other if I could help get them to communicate and trust the partnership.

Then my coaching intuition picked something else up, something I had overlooked earlier. An important element was missing in Frank's and Alison's stories about Nolan. Neither one of them had ever mentioned trying to *help* Nolan. I never heard anything about the possibility of coaching or mentoring him, so that his personal style would become less rigid. No one talked about counseling, advising or even hinting to Nolan that he might have his own communication problems.

My guess was that Nolan, like many executives I've coached, might *never* have been given straightforward feedback about his limitations. I hadn't met him yet, but I knew he deserved to hear the truth. Not only about Alison's promotion but also about why she was chosen over him.

Early in my career, I waited to be discovered. I thought my results alone would speak for themselves and the rest would take care of itself. But that wasn't how it played out. My peers were often promoted ahead of me. These were people who certainly weren't delivering better or more consistent results, yet they were seen as having more potential. I chalked it up to "politics."

So it shouldn't have been a shock when my "rival," another VP, was the first executive in the company to be selected to receive the Eagle Award for outstanding performance. But it was. I was more than shocked, I felt unappreciated and somehow betrayed. How could this political stooge, this toady be more deserving of the award than I was?

The next day I marched into the CEO's office and demanded an explanation. I was lucky. He didn't pull any punches. He said that the other executive not only was performing well in his job but also had gone beyond expectations by creating outstanding relationships with our toughest customers and suppliers. The press loved him for his accessibility, great quotes and inside knowledge of the industry. My "rival" was doing what I had convinced myself that I hated to do. I learned the hard way what all around excellence looked like in an executive position. It wasn't just the bottom line I had to manage. I needed to learn how to manage relationships as well.

There's a saying in business that great leaders are simply those who tell the truth faster. I am a great believer that in any partnership, whether it's a business, a family or a marriage, the truth serves the partnership. We can succeed so much faster when all our cards are on the table.

False flattery and fear-based positive feedback serve no one, and will often make manifest the phenomenon known as "The empty suit," referring to an executive who no longer has any real substance or competence. After years of getting only wildly positive feedback, the executive believes he is truly exceptional and supremely deserving. There is no longer any real motivation to learn or grow. Excessively arrogant and convinced of his infallibility, he sticks rigidly to his old strategies and ways of doing business. He rejects new ideas automatically. And the empty suit soon starts to fail, sometimes taking the entire company down with him. We've seen that hubris all too often in recent corporate scandals. Soon you have corporations where almost no truth at all is being told during the day.

Nolan was not exactly an empty suit yet. But because people were keeping the truth from him, he was in danger of becoming more isolated and disconnected from reality. Core skill-wise, he was a talented and capable CFO. But Nolan had stopped learning long ago. Resting on his financial laurels, he had become closed-minded about other matters. And his personal skills—skills for mediation and compromise—were sadly lacking.

I wanted Nolan to understand the promotion of Alison. I thought we might even help him see it as a chance for him to grow into the complete executive he could be. To seize this promotion as an opportunity rather than an injustice. Was I being too optimistic? Maybe so. But that's my job!

It's funny how the truth really does set us free. Reality is not our enemy. On the contrary, the paradox of reality is powerful: once people embrace it, transition almost feels effortless.

Seeking the Truth

Where are you limiting yourself? What will you do about it? Here are three steps for creating a powerful performance transition.

- *Decide to be excellent and find out what constitutes excellence in your position as well as in other positions around you and above you. Choose the position in which you would love to excel and to master. Learn as much as you can about the position.*
- *Get reliable and frequent feedback. Know where you are strong and where you have opportunities for additional growth.*
- *Choose no more than three competencies to improve each year. Select, learn, and practice a single competency until you have mastered it. Experience is the best source of development, especially in situations in which you are at risk, the stakes are high and you are stretched to your limits. Opportunities to either start something new or turn around something that is not working are examples of great developmental experiences.*

CHAPTER TEN

*In which we learn to see how problems will multiply if we
cave in to fear of confrontation.*

CONFRONTATION WITH COMPASSION

Alison, Frank and I sat in Frank's office to discuss how we were
going to roll out the news of Alison's promotion.

I looked at Alison and said, "How do you think Nolan will react
when he learns that he didn't get the promotion?"

"It'll be a real blow to his ego," she said. "Nolan thinks he's the
only real professional around here. He's always treated me like a kid
who's learning the ropes. He's not going to understand this at all.
Dad has always deferred to him when it comes to major decisions.
Believe me, he's going to be angry and feel cheated or misled."

Turning to Frank, I asked, "Was he misled?"

"Hell, no! I've never promised him a promotion or discussed a
new role for him."

Frank's answer was way too defensive. No one defends himself
so emotionally when they have inner peace about the issue. I had
learned from my own work and personal growth that I would often
automatically deny or rationalize certain behavior or motives that I
hadn't yet confronted.

Defensiveness is the first sign that you've uncovered the truth.

So I decided to press Frank a little more.

"How do you suppose that Nolan came to expect that he would
be your next COO?"

"Look, Jim, it's no secret that I've always liked and respected
Nolan. He knows this business, and he's saved our bacon more than

once. The work he did to renegotiate our loans was brilliant. Last year alone, he saw ways to improve the shop operations that ended up saving us over $1,000,000."

"And so what is it that prevented him from being the COO?"

"First of all, Jim, Alison is going to run this whole company someday soon. She's a strong leader and has proven she knows how to grow the business. She'll make a great Chief Executive Officer of this company someday, but she's not quite ready. Making her the COO is an important rounding experience. If it turns out that she doesn't want to run the company, then I will sell it. There is no point in setting up anyone else to succeed me."

"I understand, Frank, but many people make it to the CEO position without time in an operations role. Other than your development plan for Alison, is there something else stopping you from promoting Nolan?"

"Jim, you're going to find out that he is much stronger than Alison lets on. Nolan is probably the smartest man I've ever worked with. He's absolutely brilliant..."

Frank stopped to compose his thoughts. I didn't want him to stop, so I said, "But?"

Frank said, "But he's not very good with people."

"In what way?"

"He's not a strong leader. Now that I'm thinking about it, I'm not even sure that he's a strong manager when it comes to things like delegation and developing his people."

"Have you ever told him that?"

"Not in so many words." Frank paused and looked lost in his thoughts for a moment or two. "You know, Jim, I've never really given him a full appraisal or evaluation. We talk all the time, but never about interpersonal skills or leadership competencies. It never occurred to me because he is so good at the financial part of his job. Up until now, that was all that mattered to me."

People are afraid to tell the truth to each other, fearing it would cause their relationship to be damaged. But just the opposite happens. Relationships lose their bond when truth is withheld. Relationships lose all trust. Nothing feels real. Secret motives are being guessed at all day long. Fear sets in as the governing emotion in the culture.

The great business consultant Dr. W. Edwards Deming's eighth and most powerful principle was: "Drive out fear so that everyone may work effectively for the company." It was obvious that Frank's refusal to be straight with Nolan had violated that principle, and the company was paying its price.

Alison smiled at her father. "Dad, you've always laid it on pretty thick with Nolan. There hasn't been a staff meeting when you haven't complimented him or praised him for something. Nolan manages relationships up the organization better than he does down the organization."

Frank looked at me and said, "You're right, Jim. He needs to hear the truth, but there are two things I want to say about that. First, I don't want to lose him. And secondly, I'm not comfortable being the one who delivers the bad news. I hate to admit it, but I'm not very good at confronting people."

Like many people in leadership positions, Frank struggled with saying *what needs to be said*. Just as courage is a creation, so is the fear of delivering a tough message. For many of us, the source of that fear is often a story. It's a story we learned as children, usually from our parents. We learned that when we "disappointed" our parents, it appeared that we would lose their love. Sometimes they became angry and even punishing. It hurt, emotionally and sometimes physically.

Without being conscious of the thought, we can project our own story about criticism as being a form of punishment, in the way we may have experienced it earlier in our life. It is just a thought, but don't underestimate its power. I've seen it dominate people in the highest positions of authority and power—military commanders, community leaders, and Fortune 500 CEOs—who kept laggards on for years rather than confront them.

If Frank was ever to enjoy his own transition to a more peaceful level of leadership, he needed to learn a new story.

I shared with Frank what my friend and mentor, Jim Myers, had said to me when I wrestled with how to deliver bad news to a valued employee. He said that he found that he could say anything to anyone when he truly cared about the person and their well-being.

When people know you really care about them, you can say anything and they'll understand and accept the message. They may not agree, but they will listen carefully and want to know more if they trust that you have their best interests in mind.

Frank thought about that for a minute. He imagined himself talking with Nolan, speaking from his heart. He discovered that when he came from a position of care for Nolan, he found more than just courage; he found the freedom to speak the truth. He began to see that he could do this.

Frank canceled the rest of his appointments that day, and we finished the afternoon tackling a number of issues—the new accountabilities for Alison; the new organization structure, a communication plan to notify the management team, employees and key stakeholders; and how to honestly and compassionately inform Nolan.

However, we had a major psychological hurdle yet to clear. And it was a hurdle that could undo everything if we didn't clear it: What if Nolan quits?

Taking a Stand for the People You Lead

Far too many executives I coach have yet to master the art of effective feedback. They tend to either be far too harsh or much too soft. Some brag about their ability to deliver tough messages while others speak so indirectly that their people don't have a clue how they are being evaluated.

Hideo Sugiura, former Chairman of Honda Motor Co. believed that it was a "sacred obligation" of management to give fair, frequent and honest feedback so that each and every employee knows how he or she performed and how to improve.

The best leaders go beyond obligation. They take a stand for the innate ability of their people to grow professionally and personally. They know that most people have not begun to test the limits of their abilities and potential for growth. And they know that excellence does not occur without diligent and focused effort. Their gift is to build confidence by helping people be accountable, not to the leader, but to themselves for how great they can be.

Rosabeth Moss Kanter writes in her book Confidence—How Winning Streaks and Losing Streaks Begin & End *that it is the "relationship between expectations and performance that is at the heart of self-confidence...People who succeed are more likely to believe that their efforts in the future will pay off." Leadership is all about creating a compelling future and the belief it can be attained.*

CHAPTER ELEVEN

In which we learn how believing is seeing...and the process by which the mind collects all the evidence it needs to prove our most negative thoughts about others.

TRANSITION MEANS *NO FEAR*

It's not the most quoted part of his inaugural address, but one I admire greatly, when the young President John Kennedy said, "So let us begin anew—remembering on both sides that civility is not a sign of weakness, and sincerity is always subject to proof. Let us never negotiate out of fear. But let us never fear to negotiate."

One of coaching's first responsibilities is to help remove fear from any negotiation the client is entering into.

Therefore, I wanted both Frank and Alison to be completely free of the fear of losing Nolan. I knew from my own experience how that could hold them hostage to the whims of a disaffected executive.

So we looked at a number of possible outcomes, from best case to worst. Worst-case scenarios can be very liberating. I find that when people sincerely ask themselves, "What is the worst thing that could happen?" and then, "Couldn't I live with that?" their fear begins to dissipate. Soon they are on to the question, "Couldn't I even find a way to benefit from that scenario?"

So we worked to be mentally prepared should the so-called "worst" happen. We developed contingency plans if Nolan did decide to leave, and focused on creating the best outcome for both Nolan and the company.

Despite this encouraging exercise, Alison still had her doubts. She didn't trust Nolan's ability to compromise. But Frank disagreed. He said he believed that Nolan had the capability to develop better management and interpersonal skills. "He might even, if given time, make a great COO some day," said Frank.

When Alison heard that, she erupted with her well-practiced rant about what was wrong with Nolan. She had all the evidence she needed to make a case that he was totally incompetent as a leader of people.

Alison had built her case on a narrow slice of reality. She could only see what she had come to believe about Nolan—he was terrible with people.

I interrupted her and said, "Alison, I'm curious about something. During the last hour or so we listened to Frank talk about Nolan's contributions to the company—how he 'saved our bacon' more than once. Is that true?"

"Yes, but there's a whole lot more he didn't say about Nolan."

I said, "It sounds like Nolan is able to produce very significant results, even with his limited people skills. There has to be a lot more to Nolan than you're seeing now. I have a request, Alison. You don't have to do it, but are you open to at least considering a request?"

She looked at me a little suspiciously but nodded her head and said, "Okay, I'll listen."

I told her to list Nolan's greatest strengths and skills as a CFO and when she was finished writing all those down, to list her own current weaknesses and how Nolan could help her with those weaknesses.

She agreed to give it her best effort. She stood up to go to her office to work on her list and left Frank and me to work on Frank's meeting with Nolan.

My intention was to help Alison break the frozen pattern of her thinking. It is our beliefs about other people that limit our careers the most. If we can learn to challenge those beliefs at every step of the way, our careers take on a fresh vitality.

Quite often the only thing standing between my client and a successful transition to the next level of career mastery is their habit of believing every negative thought cluster that gathers. Like looking at a cloudy sky and thinking it's a permanent characteristic of the sky. Coaching, when it works, allows the clouds to pass along and the sun to eventually shine.

The Pygmalion Effect

The mind can function like a brilliant prosecuting attorney, creating an airtight case out of the most flimsy evidence. It is especially masterful in collecting evidence about other people. In The Set-Up-To-Fail Syndrome *by Jean-Francois Manzoni and Jean-Louis Barsoux we learn that the manager's perceptions of a new employee is strongly influenced by early mishaps, a former boss's evaluation and style differences. The manager then categorizes the employee as either "in" or "out." It is the category that then determines what performance evidence the manager will see in the future.*

Those who are "in" get autonomy, positive feedback and strong votes of confidence. Not surprisingly, the "outs" get micromanaged and closely controlled. Losing confidence, they lose initiative and react mechanically to being controlled, providing even more evidence of their ineptness. It happens in the office, at home and in schools.

Who is "in" and who is "out" in your life? Who have you judged as incompetent and incapable? Do they ever get better? Or do they seem to go from bad to worse? If you truly believe they are beyond redemption, you will never see the slightest degree of improved performance. If you are unwilling to look for the best in them, then fire them today and help them into their future where they can discover how good they really are.

CHAPTER TWELVE

In which we learn where excellence really comes from, and how to replace the myth of talent with the reality of practice.

THE ART OF THOROUGH PREPARATION

Frank and I sat down in his office to talk about Nolan. I asked Frank how he was feeling about the meeting. Even with a new way of thinking about giving compassionate feedback, Frank admitted that he still felt anxious and more than a little nervous when he thought about confronting Nolan. He wasn't at all deterred, but he said it would be tough for him.

"When I think about how I can help Nolan learn how to improve his effectiveness," said Frank, "I feel very confident. But when I see myself telling him about Alison's promotion, I can feel the tension building up."

Usually we find that whatever makes us think a conversation will be tough is exactly the reason to have it! I asked Frank what was tough about it for him. He threw out a number of concerns off the top of his head—things like Nolan being disappointed, upset or even angry.

I wanted to learn a little more and asked, "What might be disappointing for him?"

"Well, it's obvious. He's going to be disappointed that he didn't get the promotion."

"He could be, but I'd guess that he's probably faced that before. Like a lot of us, I suspect he's been disappointed before. Most professionals realize it's not the end of the road. What else would he be disappointed about?"

Frank thought about it for a long time, and said, "Dammit, Jim, he'll be disappointed in *me*."

"Now we're getting somewhere. Tell me how you see that."

"Well, I think I should have been straighter with him all along about my plans for Alison and the company."

"And?"

"I should have challenged him sooner. I should have talked to him about his style and not having any bench strength in his department. I should have been a better mentor and leader myself."

"Frank, those are the exact reasons to have this conversation. To be straight with Nolan and to be a strong leader and mentor for him. It's not about making him feel good about what's going on or to manipulate him into staying. It is about how you care about him and his future, and doing what you believe is best for your company."

Anyone can feel a little wobbly when he loses sight of his values and commitments, especially when emotions are running high. I wanted Frank to reconnect to his leadership role and responsibilities as the CEO.

We talked further about the true purpose of this meeting with Nolan, and when he felt he was on solid ground again, we identified the most important outcomes he wanted to produce with Nolan. He wanted Nolan to know about his plans for Alison and all the reasons for that decision, including Nolan's current limitations. He wanted Nolan to know how Frank valued him and wanted him to be a part of the company's future. He wanted him to know how he and Alison could be a great team someday. And finally, he wanted to personally help Nolan develop, but still hold him accountable for improving his leadership and interpersonal skills.

Now we were ready to put it all together. We were clear about our intended outcomes and what Frank's stand was. Although we couldn't be certain what would happen, we had brainstormed several likely reactions Nolan might have and how Frank could respond with the most integrity and serenity. We made a few notes on the key points, and then we practiced, over and over.

After about an hour, Frank felt confident and well prepared. We wrapped up, and he called Nolan to schedule time with him in the morning.

Pleased with Frank's new confidence, I stopped by Alison's office and checked on her list-making progress.

"How are you doing with the inquiries I gave you?"

"I surprised myself with the first part."

"In what way?"

"Well, Nolan *does* have a number of strengths I had never really acknowledged before. But his financial skills are already well known so that was easy. Do you want to hear what I have so far?"

"Sure, let's see what you have."

"You've already heard from Frank that Nolan is a financial wizard. And he's a tough negotiator, too. But it worries me sometimes that maybe he's too tough, you know? He also has this almost unnatural ability to remain calm and composed, even when we're in a crisis. I've never seen him totally lose his cool, and he's not afraid to make tough decisions. I mean, sometimes it irritates me, but he never seems to get rattled."

"Okay, good. What else?"

"He has a way of digging into the numbers and coming up with a solution to improve the situation—especially when it comes to manufacturing efficiencies. I don't always like the solutions, but when he makes his case it's usually airtight."

"I'm curious, Alison, how would you rate *your* financial skills? I don't mean managing your P&L, but how strong is your knowledge about cost accounting, inventory management, your balance sheet, and financing the business?"

"It's not one of my strengths. To tell you the truth, it can be a little intimidating for me. Half the time I don't understand what Nolan is talking about. I think Nolan knows it, too. He always…"

"I'm sorry. I sidetracked us there. I do want to understand the 'intimidation' part, but you were talking about the things you admire about Nolan."

"Yeah, that's right. Well, he sets very high standards for himself and everyone else. And when those standards aren't met or there is a problem, he pushes hard to correct the situation. He produces work at the highest quality levels—sometimes much higher than they need to be, if you ask me."

"What else do you see that you like about Nolan?"

"Nolan understands systems—how things interconnect and work together. He loves process improvement and analyzing workflow. It's the only time I've seen him get excited. That stuff bores me to tears, but he loves it, thank goodness. He lives and breathes 'faster, better, cheaper.' And the people in manufacturing and engineering listen to him—they may not like him, but they listen. He speaks their language."

"What do you see in all this, Alison? Is there a way he could help you to be more successful?"

"Of course he could, if we can find a way to work together. He's skilled in the areas that drain me and I don't like doing. Don't get me wrong, I know I could improve my skills in all those areas, but I don't think it's the highest and best use of my talent at this time. My job is to grow this business."

"Yes, that is your job. It's that and more. I'm willing to bet a steak dinner that as the COO you're going to find all those tools and systems that currently bore or intimidate you will be the very things you'll want to learn and master. You demanded this position because you could see the possibility of becoming the number one supplier in the nation, right? You knew that aligning sales and marketing with operations and finance was a vital factor for achieving that vision. And beginning next Monday morning after the announcements have been made, you will be accountable for accomplishing that goal. The operational excellence you want to promise your customers is now your responsibility. Oh, you're going to learn to love cost accounting and process management!"

She laughed, and relaxed into the possibility of being truly accomplished as an operational leader. I shared how many companies have achieved previously unthinkable breakthroughs in quality, time, throughput, and sales growth. There was no reason that wouldn't happen for Alison if she was willing to learn how.

I told Alison about a childhood friend of mine, Kathy Nash. Kathy and I had reconnected again in 1990 when she came to Phoenix on a consulting assignment. I learned that Kathy had been responsible for leading a revolution in supply chain management and "just-in-time" inventory for an international manufacturer of computer equipment. I say "revolution" because her work transformed the company.

Her work was so good that her company asked her to form a consulting practice to help their customers improve their operations. One of her first clients was later recognized as a Malcolm Baldridge National Quality Award recipient. Kathy's dream was to start her own practice and teach others her methodology.

When she told me about the results her team had produced, I was skeptical. Her accomplishments seemed unreal. She talked about how production had been increased tenfold; how manufacturing space was reduced by half; how quality had surpassed Japanese standards; and how cycle time was reduced from more than 40 days to a week and, eventually, to just a few hours. I was more than skeptical. I didn't think it was possible.

I told Alison that back then I wasn't ready to admit to Kathy how limited my thinking had been about quality and process management. Even though I had been driven as an executive to continuously improve, my accomplishments paled in comparison to what Kathy and her team had accomplished. So I questioned her, hoping to find out that she really wasn't really that much more effective than I was.

Kathy had faced skeptics before, and she was ready for my challenges. She explained in very simple terms how she had done it. (I've found that people who really know their subject can make it easy for anyone to understand.) She made it very easy for me. A five-year-old could have followed what she told me.

Then she sent me a list of books on the subject of time-based competition and quality. I devoured the books. As I read, I couldn't wait to put this knowledge to work. I knew it could help many companies that committed but had run out of answers for creating extraordinary results. A month later, I called Kathy and told her I would help her finance and start the consulting practice she had dreamed about.

At the time, I owned a systems integration company, but I also wanted to work closely with Kathy so I could apply and practice what I had learned. Whenever possible, I joined Kathy in her work as her apprentice. We helped a number of companies ranging from hard disk drive manufacturers to golf equipment suppliers to service companies. They all achieved results far beyond anything they had experienced before.

Quite often, in coaching, telling a story frees up the client's imagination. It allows the client some emotional distance to really hear the point. Also, it's even better when the story is one about the coach himself not being very wise or functional. It restores the coaching process to a partnership if it ever threatens to get too top heavy in the teacher-student mode.

As we spoke, Alison began to understand that Nolan was using similar approaches to what Kathy used to produce his exceptional results. She asked if I thought she could learn and use the methodologies too.

"Of course, Alison. I think you and everyone on your staff would want to learn at least the basics, but the real power in quality methods is when you put this knowledge in the hands of your front line employees. That's when the real breakthroughs start to occur."

"That will be a challenge, Jim. Knowledge is hoarded around here. The only people who ever see anything about operational metrics or financial results are Dad's management team and a few advisors."

"That's great!"

"Great? What's great about that?"

"Your job will be all about challenging the status quo. One of the first challenges we've agreed to take on is creating trust among the management team. As you get deeper into aligning the organization, you'll discover how sharing information is one of those simple yet highly effective steps to take in creating trust. And that starts with you and Nolan. I appreciate how you've already started to understand how Nolan can help you, but we haven't talked about how you will strengthen your relationship with him and the rest of the operations team."

While Alison wasn't sure how to work with Nolan, she felt confident about her ability to connect with the rest of the team. She was well aware of her ability to inspire, influence and persuade people. She had even imagined herself rallying the ops team to race to the number one position in the industry. But she knew this was a far different situation than anything she had faced before. Sometimes people stand at crossroads like these and just freeze forever. They don't see that they are always on the verge of a wonderful transition.

Not only would it be important for Alison to inspire the operations team, it would be equally important for Alison to be a trusted and credible leader. She wanted to hear more about how to go to that level.

No Shortcuts for Excellence

While it's true that certain traits like height, reaction time, intelligence or visual acuity provide an advantage, they don't provide what it takes to be outstanding and excel in your chosen field. The size of Lance Armstrong's lungs, legs and liver set him apart from many racers, but what enabled him to surpass the records of the world's greatest cyclists was painstaking work and practice. No rider before or after Armstrong's amazing seven consecutive Tour de France wins has trained as hard or demanded as much from himself than did Armstrong.

What research confirms over and over is that greatness stems from hard work and practice. Admittedly, that research doesn't explain everything about excellence. For example, it doesn't necessarily account for the savant who paints like Rembrandt at age five or who knows the exact height of a building in just a glance. And it certainly doesn't explain Armstrong's will and determination. The research does, however, clearly demonstrate that there is no substitute for consistent practice and extensive experience when it comes to extraordinary performance and overall excellence.

I know of no profession other than business leadership where practice is not the norm. When an important event is looming, like a board meeting for example, we might set aside time for a "dry run." But that's it. Business people don't practice. They say that experience is the best teacher. If that's true, why do some leaders who have given the same speech at least 50 times still sound as boring as the first time they gave it? That particular practice, giving the same boring speech 50 times, only develops the ability to comfortably give a lousy presentation. And public speaking is relatively easy compared to the real skills of business. What does it take to be outstanding in decision making, understanding and sizing up people, creativity, dealing with ambiguity and negotiating?

Sorry, but I have no silver bullet solutions here, but I do have good news. Attaining excellence in any field is within reach. It's what we've been exploring since the beginning of this book— awareness, setting goals, getting trained and practicing. It's about being coached and receiving expert feedback. It's about continually raising the bar and setting your own expectations for excellence at even higher levels. The outcome is in your hands and always has been.

CHAPTER THIRTEEN

In which we learn that before the team will freely join you and give their best effort, you must earn their trust.

TRANSITION PARTNERS WITH REALITY

Far too many new leaders try to inspire their new team with lofty goals and dramatic change. Having just read *Good to Great*, the executive assembles the troops and gives an impassioned speech about all the great things they'll accomplish together.

The problem is that the people know they aren't even "good" yet, much less ready to be great. Without knowing it, the new leader is creating a roomful of cynics. Because he doesn't have a clue about their reality, he is trying to force a transition before its time.

Alison was not only new and an outsider to the operations team, she was also perceived as the "enemy." She and her sales team had been demanding the impossible for years. As far as operations were concerned, she just didn't get it. Like it or not, Alison did not have credibility with the operations team. No matter how inspiring Alison might be, the team would not be able to hear what they didn't yet believe.

In my own life as a company executive, I'd been in that position. I'd been in front of more than one roomful of people who sat with their arms crossed, already doubting me before I opened my mouth. I knew what it felt like. I knew the wall that had to come down.

It didn't take me long to learn a more effective approach. Rather than start with the usual meetings and pronouncements, I learned to spend my first two weeks on the factory floor. But first, I would briefly meet with my management team and let them know what I was up to. The word spread quickly and it was no surprise when I came in with the first shift the next day.

Even though I had dressed in a tee shirt, jeans and an old pair of running shoes, I was recognized right away. The people on the front lines can easily spot a "suit" trying to mix in. A number of them walked up and introduced themselves and put me at ease right away. I worked in the lowest skilled job, an entry-level material handler. That meant my only job was to serve the technicians who were configuring the systems. If they wanted something, I got it for them. If they needed something moved, I moved it for them. If they wanted something picked up, I picked it up.

I listened and I learned. I shadowed the floor supervisors and the operations managers, observing their daily routines. I followed a sales order through the system, from the time it was entered until the time it shipped. I sat in on staff meetings and planning sessions. It was like a cultural immersion in a foreign country. It didn't take me long to learn their language and customs. And I rapidly got a good feel for the operation—strengths, weaknesses and opportunities for improvement.

Uninformed and naïve, I experienced the new operation without any preconceived notions. I was very curious and asked a lot of questions. I didn't have any stories, excuses or rationalizations about why things were the way they were. That allowed me to see things the management team had overlooked for years. I looked for the constraints that were uninvestigated and untested—the ones that no one had challenged.

It was like visiting a distant relative's home and noticing the different smells, the stains on the sofa and scratches on the kitchen cabinets that had become a comfortable part of their environment. The same smells, stains and scratches we have in our homes but have long since stopped noticing. My first 90 days became peak learning experiences and set the stage for a successful transition.

I believed Alison's success would largely be predicated by the effectiveness of her first 90 days on the job. There are three common reasons why star performers fail in new positions: 1) Not fitting in with the culture; 2) Management style differences; and 3) Poor relationships with peers, their staff and key stakeholders.

Alison would be challenged by all three.

Alison listened quietly as I told her my story about gaining credibility by learning and living inside other people's reality. I had covered a lot of ground, so I checked in with her and asked what she had heard. I was convinced as I sat listening to her that she had taken it all in and made it her own.

She decided to start after the announcements were made on Monday morning by meeting with everyone either one-on-one or in small groups. Rather than tell people what she wanted, she would ask a lot of questions and listen carefully.

We created an agenda for her initial one-on-one meetings with her new operations staff. I helped her craft some questions that were designed to help people open up and reduce their defensiveness. After introducing herself and saying a little about her background, values, style and aspirations, she would ask the following:

1. Tell me about yourself: brief bio and your school years, your family, how long with the company, and your previous work experience.
2. Tell me what you most enjoy about being a part of the operations team.
3. In what areas are you most skilled? What do you really enjoy doing most?
4. What accomplishments are you most proud of?
5. What are your top goals this year?
6. What is it that you are not very good at doing? What do you really dislike doing? What drains you?
7. Let's say Frank made you the COO of this organization and gave you the authority to take any action as long as it made us a better company. What are the first three things you would change?
8. Where else do you see some interesting opportunities?
9. If I were a fly on the wall at your home during dinner, what might I overhear you express over dinner after a really tough day on the job? What frustrates you the most?

10. How can I help you be more successful?
11. How can you help me be more successful? I want to learn more about manufacturing, process, quality and costs.
12. What else should I know?

We agreed to meet later that week and create her 90-day plan based on what she learned in those meetings. That would include things like an immersion in operations, connecting and creating strong relationships with her team and Nolan, and finally crafting her top objectives.

We still had one more challenge to tackle before we called it a night—her relationship with Nolan, assuming he chose to stay with the company after his meeting with Frank.

When I brought that final subject up, Alison looked flustered. "Jim, I'm stuck on how to create a trusting relationship with Nolan, or even a civil one for that matter."

"It may be hard to see now," I said, "but that may have more to do with you than it does Nolan. Can we set aside your current view of the situation for a while? We won't forget about it. We'll just set it aside for a minute and look at another scenario, okay?"

Alison was ready for anything. I said, "Let's take the case that Frank's meeting with Nolan goes well tomorrow, even better than we planned. Nolan trusts that he is valued and has a role in the company's future, at least as the CFO. He also understands Frank's concerns about his leadership. Even if he doesn't agree right away, let's say he wants to learn more and do something about it. Can you see that as a possibility?"

"Yes."

"Good! Frank has made it clear that his dream is for you and Nolan to be a powerful team, working together to make this a great company. How will you contribute to that? How will you create a relationship with Nolan that results in trust and mutual respect so that you can be that kind of team?"

Alison said nothing.

"I am inviting you to think about this seriously. If you can't commit to serving Nolan and helping him succeed, then you may not be ready for this position. As the president, one of your most important jobs will be to develop talent and help people be the best they can be. That includes people like Nolan."

Alison started writing notes.

I said, "I would like you to imagine yourself creating a relationship with Nolan that has him trusting you enough to help you and to ask for help himself. How would you create that? Will you think about that for me tonight?"

Alison said she would, but reluctantly. I sensed that her current reality was preventing her from seeing any more positive possibilities. I decided that we had had enough coaching for one day.

As we started to leave her office, I said, "Sometimes I find I can create the most innovative solutions when I look at the problem as if I was the cause of it. It doesn't matter if that's really true or not. I just find more power to create and more freedom to act when there's nobody else to blame but me and nobody else to fix it but me. If I am responsible and accountable for everything that happens, then it's up to me to find a solution."

Alison looked interested.

I decided to continue in this vein, "It's probably not true, but what if you learned that *you were the cause* of the relationship you have with Nolan? What if it had nothing to do with Nolan at all? How would you restore that relationship? Are you willing to take on the responsibility for moving the relationship forward?"

Alison looked at me in a new way, with a mixture of hope and curiosity. I realized I had created some space for her to think in a way that wasn't fixated on Nolan being wrong.

Become a Trusted Leader

When do you trust someone? When don't you trust? How people answer these questions doesn't vary that much. It usually boils down to the degree of certainty one has about another person's actions in the future. It is the same thing that drives the Dow Jones Industrial Average and why one stock sells at a higher multiple of earnings than do other stocks. It has to do with the reliability of predicted performance. The more accurate the prediction, the greater the trust becomes.

People will not follow you if they don't trust you. They will not freely give their hearts and minds to your cause if they can't rely on you. Posner and Kouzes, authors of The Leadership Challenge *offer a simple solution—DWYSYWD—Do What You Say You Will Do.*

It sounds easy, doesn't it? But unless we are fully conscious and present to our thoughts and words, we may be breaking our word every day. It's the little things that start chronic cynicism. We say, "I'll start the meeting at 10:00," but show up at 10:09. We say, "I'll call back in a week," but don't call for a month. We say, "I'll review you on your anniversary date," but are three months late with the review. Has the contraction "I'll" lost its meaning? Do we use it to avoid saying "I will" out loud? Because "I will" is a promise, a precise commitment of future action. What does "I'll" mean to you?

CHAPTER FOURTEEN

In which we learn how to replace the fear of being proven wrong with the practice of getting to the truth of the matter.

WINNING RESPECT AND CREDIBILITY

I didn't have anything to base it on, but I had a hunch that Nolan wouldn't resign.

The next morning Alison, Frank and I met to review Frank's meeting with Nolan. Frank said he was satisfied with the meeting, but was not exactly sure how well Nolan took the news of Alison's promotion.

"What do you mean by that, Frank?" I asked.

"Well, Nolan didn't say all that much," Frank said. "He didn't really display any emotion, which isn't unusual for him, but still. You know what the toughest part was?"

Alison and I were silent, but nodded for him to continue.

"The toughest part was acknowledging my own role in not being more straightforward."

Alison said, "How did Nolan react to that?"

"Oh, he let me off the hook by saying he understood. He admitted that he wasn't great with people, but he disagreed with me about his leadership ability. Nolan said he had always seen himself as a strong leader."

I asked, "How did you leave it?"

Frank said, "Nolan committed himself to support Alison and said he was open to learning more about his leadership weaknesses. I offered to place him in the same leadership-coaching program that Alison has with you, but he wasn't sure about that. He said he'd like some time to think about it. But he did ask to meet with several of the outside advisory board members and get their feedback as well."

We all agreed that Nolan's response didn't give Alison much to work with. She asked me how she should approach Nolan.

I think she already knew the answer.

But I responded by saying, "Let's start with the inquiry I gave you last night. What did you come up with?"

Alison said, "I'm not ready to admit that this is all my problem, but I did what you asked me to do. What I saw is not a pretty picture. I have been fighting with Nolan since the day Dad hired him. There was something about his style that irritated me the first time I met him. I think it was because he didn't seem to trust me. And then later on when Dad started to praise him, I felt jealous and threatened."

"Why do you think you felt that way?"

"I had always been the star around here. So I argued with Nolan in staff meetings and tried to make him look bad. If he used logic, I responded with anger. If he asked for data, I demanded a decision. If he wanted facts and figures, I came back with customer demands and competitive information. I fought him every way I could, even when I knew he was right."

"That's a pretty good place to start, Alison!" I said. "Start by sincerely acknowledging how you behaved and why. Apologize and ask what you can do to make it work with him. Finish by asking for his support in moving the company forward. Make it as honest and heartfelt as you can. You may find it very tempting to use that meeting to review your grievances with Nolan. If it were me, I would resist doing that. First, that is not our objective for this meeting. And, more important, over the next several weeks your perceptions of Nolan will probably change. You will start to experience him in a whole new light, especially if you are sincere in your commitment to partner with him."

Later that day Alison met with Nolan. It was a meeting that went surprisingly well. As he did with Frank, Nolan made it easy for Alison. He accepted her apology and offered his own. He assured her that he was a professional and would continue to perform his job to his highest ability. She shared her dreams for the company's future and her plans to meet with the management team. She promised to share her findings with Nolan and get his input before making any decisions. It was clear that a truce had broken out.

When she asked Nolan what she could do to make their partnership work better, he opened up further and explained that he didn't like surprises, especially in staff meetings. He needed time to process and analyze new information. What would help most would be if Alison would discuss her proposed initiatives with him before the meeting.

It was a simple enough request and Alison readily agreed. What neither of them foresaw was how much those meetings would help align them. As they met with each other they still tended to debate and defend their own viewpoints. But instead of trying to make one or the other wrong, the debate would now be about what was best for the company. Because these were private discussions, there was no audience for either of them to play to. They could focus on each other instead of worrying about group approval.

In my coaching work I have found that getting two people together often has magical, unintended results. If I can get two warring people to commit to meet with each other regularly, it is miraculous how quickly they transition out of fear and resentment into a new spirit of partnership.

These meetings were also an opportunity for Nolan to show Alison how he analyzed proposals. As the days went by, Alison learned a lot and so did Nolan. He was impressed by her insight and market knowledge. She often pointed out a number of factors Nolan tended to omit in his analysis. He even had to admit that after his analysis, her hunches were usually right on.

Soon the two of them were meeting weekly. If one of them was traveling, they scheduled a call instead.

Nolan could see how Alison was consciously modifying her behavior. She was more patient with him and came to their meetings well prepared. She started to read and rely on Nolan's extensive monthly reports. He appreciated how she was spending every Friday on the factory floor learning every step of the operation. Alison enrolled in an intensive two-week executive financial course at a leading graduate school and followed that with an executive course on the Six Sigma process. She finally understood that as far as credible leadership is concerned, knowledge is power.

I continued to coach Alison during her first six months in the COO role. After a few months, she came into one of our meetings one day and appeared a little less energized than usual. I asked what was on her mind. She said that since we had last met, her arguments with Nolan had heated up again.

The honeymoon was over.

"Nolan is fighting me again," she said. "Especially about my plans to grow the business. He just doesn't have the vision that I do. I'm tempted to just go over his head and take it to my father. I know I can get his support to move ahead with my plans if I push hard enough."

"What's stopping you?" I asked.

"I've worked hard to earn Nolan's trust. I don't want to destroy the little I've gained by going over his head. Besides, Frank has taken a pretty neutral stance and seems to be turning most of the decision making over to Nolan and me. But I want to move faster than Nolan's willing to."

"Alison, you're learning what I and almost every new senior leader I know has had to learn. We come into a new executive level position expecting at least an equal amount of increased power, authority and control. After all, we're now responsible for delivering bigger results than ever before. But then reality bites, and we learn that our ability to produce results is directly tied to our ability to influence, inspire and enroll others who have competing interests. What had looked like automatic power and control in other leaders turned out to have been hard-won. It may have been more about their character, emotional intelligence, and ability to manage diverse relationships."

Alison understood immediately. She was already advanced in her relationship skills. But Nolan remained a perplexing challenge for her. The good news was that they were still talking and meeting every week. As a way to end the stalemate, Alison asked if I would help facilitate a healthy discussion between them about their impasse. I agreed to help, but only after privately meeting with Nolan and hearing his side of the problem.

We were on the verge of a final transition, and I didn't want to get careless and leave Nolan out of the equation.

A Clash of Egos

You've heard it before. Two people arguing about something in which both had equally justifiable points. But their emotions had escalated far beyond the worthiness of the matter being argued. What's the argument really about? If you listen carefully, you might hear a desperate fight about being right.

Most of us learned at an early age that being right got us what we wanted most—love, inclusion, and approval. Some even say the need to be right may not only come from early conditioning but also from a primitive tribal instinct. It wasn't too long ago when the cost of not fitting in or not doing things the "right way" led to being cast out. And that meant certain death. Even in more modern times the consequences include torture or a gruesome death.

If that's true, then maybe the need to be right could be nothing more than a primitive reaction to survive. Check it out for yourself. How do you react when you're given advice you didn't ask for? What about when someone interrupts you and supplies additional information before you've finished making your point? Do you notice any resistance? Do you immediately seek to understand or do you defend yourself?

I caught myself just last week. I was sharing an important concept with a client when he interrupted and mentioned reading something that slightly contradicted the point I was making. Rather than stop and ask about it, I nodded signifying I heard him and continued making my point, but much more energetically than necessary. Why? In that moment, I was more interested in being right than learning something new—something that might prove me wrong.

Clinging desperately to the need to be right has derailed many formerly successful people. Their outdated concepts and self-limiting beliefs trap them in irrelevance. I continue to learn, usually in very humbling ways, what a gift it is to discover when I am wrong. That discovery is the key to all successful transitions and personal growth.

CHAPTER FIFTEEN

In which we learn to replace fear of the unknown with a powerful sense of purpose.

THE FINAL ROADBLOCK IS ALWAYS FEAR

As I took a seat in Nolan's office and told him that I wanted to facilitate a meeting with him and Alison, I could see that he was not too happy about the idea.

"You don't look too pleased by the prospect of a meeting with the three of us," I said.

"I'm a little skeptical," Nolan said.

"What about?"

"I just doubt that you can be entirely neutral," he said.

"Because?"

"Because you're Alison's coach. You are very close to her."

"I appreciate your directness," I said. "Why don't you and I talk for awhile, and when we're through I won't facilitate the meeting unless I've gained your full support and commitment. This meeting has to be a good idea for you, too." Roadblocks to transition show up as many different things. But beneath every one is fear.

So Nolan and I kept talking.

It didn't take long to connect with Nolan. When he understood that I was only there to learn and not to convince him about anything, he began to share his perspective about Alison, her promotion and their relationship.

He told me that it had been very difficult for him when Frank told him about promoting Alison. He felt blindsided, and even betrayed at first. He didn't see it coming. He knew, of course, that

Alison wanted more control, and rumor had it that she was angling for the COO position. But he truly believed he had the inside track for the job.

"Do you still believe that?" I said.

"Believe what?"

"That you should be the COO."

"Yes, I do think I'm the right man for that job. And I still hope I will be the President and COO of this company someday. In fact, I'd love to be the CEO when the time is right. But I knew this was a family-owned business when I came here and these kinds of things happen."

"How do you mean 'these kinds of things happen'?"

"I mean that it's more likely that a family member will succeed Frank as the CEO. I had always thought it might be his younger brother who has a law practice and sits on the advisory board. But I didn't think that would prevent me from stepping into the COO position."

"Nolan, how do you see things today? How do you rate Alison's performance?"

"She's surprised me. I've never seen anyone work harder, and she is coming up to speed much more quickly than I thought she would. We're ahead of plan now, and she wants to keep it going."

"So, what's the problem?"

Nolan said, "What she doesn't understand is that we don't have the working capital to sustain the kind of growth she wants. She has already blown the expense budget for this quarter and if sales suddenly drop off we may not make our profit plan. And the profit plan is my accountability. If we make or exceed plan, I keep my job and get a nice bonus. If we don't, then...well, let's just say I better keep my resume current."

I could finally sense the depth of Nolan's fear. When coaching is most effective it is usually because a fear has been revealed and understood. In fact, in my experience, fear is the only real problem anyone has.

But what I wasn't able to discern at that time was if Nolan was truly obstructing Alison. If he was, was it a subversive act of self-preservation, or was it in the best interest of the company? Was the company truly capital constrained? Was Alison pushing the company beyond a healthy growth rate? Was her zeal an act of ego and "irrational exuberance" or a rational competitive response to the market conditions?

As I continued my conversation with Nolan it also became clear that Nolan, Alison and Frank were not aligned on the business's overall purpose or strategy. By business purpose, I don't mean vision or mission. I mean the reason for being in the business.

Originally, it had been because Frank and his partner had sold their framing business during a building slump. They didn't want to go to work for anybody else so they explored other options in the construction industry. They decided to get into a new line of business that was less volatile and could easily be expanded on a regional basis. That led them to supplying custom doors and cabinets for luxury homes.

But that was twenty-five years ago. What was the purpose now? Was it to create a legacy business for the family? Was it to create wealth? Or was it to contribute to the greater good, providing jobs and support for the community? What was the end game now? That was a question that had not been asked nor answered for years.

I knew that unless we had an answer to that question, the team would eventually fall apart. With no central purpose, the road to transition is always blocked, and teams are always at cross-purposes.

The final piece of this puzzle was now on the table.

Business Purpose

Most businesses, large and small, are started with the sense of adventure, energy and high expectations. They are always started with a purpose in mind—perhaps to make a living or even create wealth. Many entrepreneurs are driven by a quest for personal freedom and a means to express their talent. Others may start with a loftier purpose, one that will make a difference for all stakeholders and contribute to the greater good. No matter what the original purpose is, all businesses will be challenged by the same problem. At some point the adventure loses energy and expectations become a boring routine. Purpose has been lost or is no longer relevant.

If a business is not driven by a compelling purpose, then fear rules the business. Without purpose, the leadership team is unable align, collaborate or make major decisions. Managers withdraw into their silos, fiercely protecting their turf. The business is governed by meaningless metrics designed to avoid looking bad. The only real goal is survival or not to lose whatever is left of value. Aimless and without a driving force, the business stagnates.

A business, whether it has one employee or thousands, is created by human spirit, creativity and will. The business' ability not only to survive but to thrive is determined by the extent to which its people are given the opportunity to fully engage and contribute to a cause that connects with their own spirit, values and life purpose. What about your business? Are the people energized, engaged and contributing? If not, first take a look at your own leadership, values, and vision before you question the lack of engagement of your team.

Chapter Sixteen

In which we learn how to align with others and share a powerful sense of purpose so that the impossible now becomes possible.

How the Truth Will Set You Free

No one had even questioned the reason for growing the business in the first place. Why grow the business? Would growing the business serve a strategic need? If so, how fast and how much? Was growth an expression of Alison's spirit? Or was it merely her idea for a good time?

Alison believed she could grow the business organically, taking market share through customer penetration, developing new products and geographic expansion. Nolan thought that would create a price war and that the only rational way to grow the business was through acquisitions, but only if they could get financing. Frank sat on the fence, seeing the pros and cons of both strategies.

No wonder they found themselves sinking back into heated arguments. There could be no resolution to an argument that had no basis for a meaningful conclusion. Adding to the friction was their opposing behavioral styles and attitudes.

This required more than one facilitated discussion. It was time for Nolan and Alison to confront the reality of their situation and expose the misunderstandings they had each created. It was time for both of them to act in the best interest of the company and each other. And it was time to for Frank and the board to provide leadership and direction for the management team.

We scheduled a meeting that Saturday morning at my office. After setting the ground rules and establishing our objectives, I started by asking them each to share their dreams for the company.

Alison's vision was to have a fast-moving, fast-growing agile company that would be the industry leader.

Nolan spoke his own vision of an operationally excellent and very profitable company.

The more they talked, the more their visions converged. The question started to dawn on all of us: Why can't we be both? Why not be fast moving *and* operationally excellent?

I stood at the white board capturing the points they agreed on. I am a believer in writing dreams and visions down. It makes them real. It makes them clear and visible. I wanted them all up there on the white board to keep the possibility of what *could be* in front of us when we examined the current reality.

I shifted our focus to Nolan and Alison working together and bringing that possibility forward. We looked at their individual strengths, talents and gifts as well as their current weaknesses and self-limiting beliefs. They immediately saw how complementary they could be.

I had my own vision about the possibility of their relationship. Few leaders possessed the combination of all the gifts Nolan and Alison held individually. Working together, they could be an unstoppable force. Working against each other, they could be a destructive force.

It was their choice.

They agreed and wanted to understand what was in their way. I decided to take a risk. I asked them to create a list of the three to five things that irritated them the most about each other and share it.

Their conversation was a guarded one at first. They started with the easiest things on their list. Alison said that when Nolan was under pressure he was "a pessimistic, picky perfectionist who was impossible to please." Nolan countered that when Alison was stressed, she was "…unrealistic and glib. She talked too much without saying anything meaningful."

And because they didn't know about each other's personal values and motives, they did what most uninformed people do—

they created stories based on their perceptions of the other person's behavior and then collected evidence to prove how right their stories were and how wrong the other person was.

They both opened up a little more as soon as I pointed out that their irritations with each other were reactions to an overplayed strength—the same strengths that they were just admiring in each other minutes ago.

The fast mover in Alison was frustrated with the deliberate thinking of Nolan. The deliberate thinker in Nolan did not trust the fast mover's lack of facts. The artful communicator in Alison was irked by the direct and blunt style of Nolan. Their strengths, under stress, became perceived weaknesses.

We were making good progress seeing these insights, but neither of them had yet talked about what they had shared with me privately. So I asked if there was anything else they wanted to say. The room was quiet. No one spoke. It was their decision. They knew what was at stake.

Finally Alison said what she came to say. "Nolan, I think you have been undermining me. I think you want me to fail and prove that you should have been the COO. You come up with all the necessary logic about why we shouldn't grow so fast, but we both know the real reasons you're fighting me. You want my job."

Nolan took a deep breath and said, "It is true that I'd like to be COO. But the last thing I want is for you to fail. If you fail, I fail. Let's face the facts. First of all, you are Frank's daughter and he's not going to fire you. If anyone is gets fired for financial problems, it will be me. And I don't want to lose my job. I believe in this company, and I want to be a part of its future."

I asked Alison if she could accept what Nolan had said. She didn't answer right away. She stared into Nolan's eyes. It was a meaningless gesture, she already believed him. She just needed a way to end it. "Thank you, Nolan. I accept that. "

I asked Nolan if he had anything else he wanted to say.

"I've said it all before. We don't need to grow this business much more than five to ten percent a year."

Alison cut him off. "Five percent? I might as well…"

I interrupted her. "Alison, this is important. Please listen and let him finish."

I could see that she didn't expect that from me. Surely her supportive coach would understand how right she was about Nolan.

I said, "Most recurring arguments are not about being right. They are about being heard and understood. It's possible that Nolan is covering this ground again because he doesn't feel that he is being understood. I'm not saying that he is right or wrong. You don't have to agree with him, just listen and understand where he is coming from."

Nolan went on and explained how their previous rate of sales and profitability was producing more than acceptable returns to the owners. At a moderate growth rate, they could continue healthy growth without borrowing money or raising equity capital. They had perfected a simple business model that was self sustaining and easy to manage. Why put that at risk?

He then said that he didn't like some of the financial trends that were developing under Alison's leadership. Over the last sixty days margins had slipped and the finished goods inventory was building up. The new products weren't selling as fast as Alison had forecasted. Some of the large dealers that Alison's team had recently signed on were known to be slow payers and tough negotiators. It wouldn't be long before they would have cash flow problems.

And to top it off, Nolan said, Alison was exceeding her budget every month and she still wanted more money for new collateral material. The new dealers thought their existing brochures and displays were outdated and hokey. Their existing dealers seemed to be happy with what they had. He didn't see any reason to bow to the demands of the new dealers.

He finished by saying, "Alison, can't you see where this is going? You're putting the company in a dangerous situation. If this keeps up, you'll ruin what it took Frank 25 years to build. And what frustrates me the most is that I don't think I can stop you. You're going to do what you want no matter what and that scares the hell out of me."

So there it was. Two executives without a common purpose, holding opposing goals and fighting to be right. One was fearless and out to win at any cost. The other feared failure and played not to lose.

You would have to be unconscious not to discern the shift in the energy in the room. In less than an hour, they had experienced the exhilaration of the future they could create together and the draining foolishness of their current reality.

I sat there, not saying anything. There comes a time in coaching when you need to release your agenda. A coach can't force a transition. You need to give up control and just watch. And trust that whatever happened next would be exactly what needed to happen.

It wasn't long before Alison said, "I *could* tell you why we need to push hard and take more market share, but I won't. I don't think it will help. So, now what do we do?"

I said, "Okay, then, Alison, what do you want to do now?"

"I want to get back to the possibility we created together this morning," she said. "It was powerful and uplifting. I think we could get back there if we wanted to. What do you think, Nolan?"

Nolan didn't react right away. It was obvious that he needed time to process his thoughts. I asked him if he could think out loud for a minute so Alison could understand where he was coming from.

"Okay," Nolan said. "I know that by agreeing to move ahead we might find some common ground again. It seems logical."

I could tell that Nolan was still wrestling with risking the simple but effective business model he had created. He could agree, but he wanted to put conditions on it first.

It felt like it was time for me to get back in the conversation.

"It's a little early to set limits on your future, Nolan. There will be plenty of time to do that, and I'm going to tell you how we can do that. But for now, can you get behind the possibility that you and Alison created for the company this morning?"

I pointed to the white board. He studied it again. All Nolan's ideas for excellence had been captured. And when his ideas were combined with Alison's, the possibility was compelling and hard to resist. They both wanted to build a legacy company, something that would last for generations.

I shared my thoughts about how it was time for them to align with Frank and refresh the business purpose. They could start by bringing Frank what they had discovered about themselves and their future and ask for his support. Once they all agreed on the long-term outcomes and when they wanted to achieve them, the rest would be relatively easy.

Over the next several weeks, the three of them hammered out a rough plan to grow the business to a size that would allow them to remain independent, even as the big box stores like Home Depot and Lowe's were becoming more dominant in their market. It looked like they could hang on to their niche and still triple the size of the business. If they couldn't sustain their share, they would be an attractive acquisition target.

Nolan and Alison pulled their teams together and went to work on the sales and operations plans. That gave Nolan the visibility he needed to understand the capital requirements to support the growth. Alison had a road map, big goals to accomplish and a set of guidelines to operate within. And she had the authority and resources she needed to do the job. Alison was ready to roll.

But there was a surprise in store for them.

As Nolan finalized the plans, he reached an unexpected conclusion. When he understood what tripling the size of the business meant, he saw that neither he nor Alison had the expertise needed to lead an operation of that magnitude. It was already a handful to manage.

He called me and we met for lunch. He wasn't sure how to handle this new discovery. The implications seemed to be clear. They would need to hire a very experienced COO soon, probably in a year or so. Should he go to Frank and Alison and tell them what he'd found?

"Is there a reason not to?" I asked. "It seems like that's something you'd want to resolve right away."

His ego was telling him that he could develop as a leader and learn enough to do that job himself someday. That had always been his dream. The timing could work out if Alison stepped up to the CEO role in a couple of years. But something was telling him to let it go. When he really thought about it, he wasn't sure if that was right for him.

That was unsettling for Nolan. He didn't like being filled with doubt. Couldn't it be disruptive to have another executive on the team? Shouldn't he strive to be the best he could be? Wasn't it wrong not to reach for the next level? Was he just giving up? What would Frank think?

I smiled at him and said, "I've had those same questions rattle around in my head before, too. But let's look at something you said a minute ago. You said you weren't sure that being the COO under those conditions was right for you. Tell me more."

I wanted to understand if he was running away from something he feared or moving toward something he wanted. When you understand the fear, you understand everything.

He said he had never enjoyed his work more than he had during the last month. He loved the planning, the analysis and putting together the capital plan. He was energized when he huddled with Frank and Alison and helped design the future. They trusted him and listened to him. He was making contributions every day.

I said, "Do you know how powerful that is? That doesn't limit who you are or what your possibilities are in the future. It does the opposite. You just opened up a whole new future. When you come to work every day with that spirit of belonging and contribution, you break through the limits of roles and titles. Can you see how limited you were when you were so attached to the COO position? When you truly were intending to help, you were resisted. People stopped listening. Alison fought you, even when she could see you were right. The more you were resisted, the more you tried to control people. What you thought you wanted most kept getting further away."

Maybe that's what Joseph Campbell meant by "follow your bliss." It has nothing to do with resignation or retreat. It has everything thing to do with loving what you do, being fully engaged and contributing. The rest takes care of itself.

I don't know why it works that way. But I love that it does. I can't get enough of what I crave, yet I receive enough of everything I love.

Nolan didn't get the promotion. I helped Frank and Alison select a great new COO who started contributing immediately. (Several months after the new COO started, Nolan confided that he still wished he had been chosen to be the COO. But he can now see it was his ego talking. Today he is doing the work he was meant to do—and doing so happily as the CFO.)

Alison was promoted to the CEO position, and she and Nolan still meet every week. They've successfully completed their transition to becoming a great team. Because they've built in a system for understanding each other.

Aligning with Integrity

Are you free to say what must be said? Do you fully express yourself, even in the most dicey and professionally risky situations? A clue to the degree to which you fully express yourself is how you feel after a conversation. Are you still processing the conversation, playing it over and over in your mind? Do you feel lingering resentment or anger? If so, you still have something to say.

I can still remember when as a young executive I became acutely aware of what I left unsaid. The CEO and I were meeting on a regular basis, and there were days when I left that meeting feeling totally energized and engaged; and there were times when I left thinking about the letter of resignation I would write. What was the difference? Ultimately it proved to be whether or not I had the integrity, courage and clarity to reach closure with the CEO.

I was fortunate to have a friend who suggested that I replay and rewrite those uncomfortable encounters in my mind, seeing myself artfully and graciously expressing what needed to be said. What happened next was surprising. After a meeting with my CEO, I was immediately struck with the thought that my business wasn't finished. I turned around, went back to his office and said, somewhat sheepishly, that I had one or two things more to say. That happened randomly for several months, becoming an inside joke between us. Gradually, my awareness shifted, and I was able to catch myself in the moment. I developed the capacity to stay in the conversation until we were both complete. I can't think of anything else in our long relationship that bonded us more closely than straight talk.

If you want to test this, take fifteen minutes at the end of each day and review your conversations for a week or two. Think about what you had intended to say and what was actually said. Try to remember your reaction to what was being said and what you were thinking the moment before you spoke. How connected were you with the other person. Did you listen? I mean really listen. When you truly listen and connect, you don't notice your own thoughts. At the most, you might notice the ebb and flow of your emotions. At the end of the day, how do you feel about the quality of your conversations—energized, confident and complete? If not, go back and say what needs to be said. Reclaim your integrity.

CHAPTER SEVENTEEN

In which we learn why leadership exists only in conversations—words, ideas and thoughts—and why the only action a leader takes is to communicate.

CONVERSATIONS CREATE TRANSITIONS

I was very heartened that Nolan had chosen to become a creative contribution to the company, and not shoot himself in the foot by continuing his opposition to Alison.

The phrase, "Shooting one's self in the foot," is usually attributed to the ironically unintended consequence of a well-intended act. Like the DEA agent who accidentally and literally shot himself in the foot while teaching gun safety to a classroom of children and their parents.

But it's not always an accident. I think the phrase originated during wartime, when a soldier would "accidentally" wound himself in order to get out of a battlefield situation. So "shooting yourself in the foot" can be a way to take yourself out of action without killing yourself. I've seen many executives, especially those who have become disengaged, take themselves out of action.

One of my clients recently called about a talented executive on his senior staff. I'll call him Jerry. He was about to get himself fired. Jerry had made several bad decisions and had dropped the ball more than once on an important project. When confronted, his response was defensive, and he had a long list of excuses blaming others for his shortfall.

It's instructive to watch people who are trying to covertly fire themselves. This is actually a negative, subconscious form of transitioning! In a marriage relationship or in a business relationship, it's all the same. They want to bring the issue of their sense of disconnect to a head, but they want someone else to do it for them. They want someone else to be the one to bring them to a crossroads.

They aren't willing to truthfully communicate about whether they really want to be doing this work any longer. They don't want to go up on the mountain and fast for forty days and come back with an answer. They want someone else to tell them "you should probably leave" and so they covertly generate the conflict that forces the issue.

People shoot themselves in the foot to avoid the courage that leadership is asking of them in the moment. Jerry did that. Believing he was being stretched beyond his capability, he created an unnecessary conflict with the CEO. It gave him the escape route he was looking for. If fired, he could justify it because of how intolerable his relationship with the CEO had become. Anyone could see that, right?

A lot of research has been done on why good executives suddenly leave companies. Most often cited are things like not enough challenge or opportunity for growth, or sometimes it's a lack of appreciation, trust or cultural fit. But I have to wonder if those are the real causes. If an executive is truly "good," then it seems like a lack of challenge or growth could be easily resolved. What's missing here? Could it be as simple as an open and honest conversation?

Jerry and his CEO never had a completely honest conversation until the day Jerry was fired. The CEO believed that Jerry's technical abilities were rare and could not be easily replaced. He felt threatened by the thought of losing Jerry and never directly confronted Jerry's poor performance. Jerry continued to defend his poor performance and lack of accountability. He never admitted to his CEO that he was in over his head and needed help.

In the movie "Philadelphia," Denzel Washington played a lawyer who would get to the bottom of something by saying "Now, explain it to me like I'm a four-year-old." He wanted it simply and clearly, but it can be hard to get it that way when people are afraid to speak the truth.

After I saw that movie, I started thinking how it would be to experience the business world through the eyes of a child. Let's say that a leader takes her four-year-old, Timmy, to the office. Timmy is well behaved and tags along watching Mommy in action as a leader. When they get home, her spouse asks Timmy what happened.

Timmy says, "Nothing much. We sat around a lot. Sometimes we were alone and sometimes we were at a big table with other people. I think they were mad or sad or something. Mommy talked on the phone or typed on the computer. Sometimes we just walked around and said hello to people. It was kind of boring. Mommy said it was hard to be the boss. She was tired."

So, if we watch a leader take action through the eyes of a four-year-old, what do they do? Pick up the phone. Talk to someone. Send an email. Create a plan. Write a letter or a proposal. Go see someone. Leaders communicate. That's their only job. A simple act that looks like nothing but creates everything.

It's the door they choose to walk through in the mornings, who they greet on their way in, and the expressions on their faces…everything…everything about them is a conversation. But leaders themselves often don't see this. They lose the sense that their leadership is manifested in how and what they are communicating!

The great ontological philosopher Heidegger said, "Language is the house of Being. In its home man dwells. Those who think and those who create with words are the guardians of this home." Obviously, the super CFO Nolan missed the whole communication piece, which is why his transition to a higher leadership position never happened.

If I look at my worst mistakes as a leader, they always occurred because of the things that I said or didn't say in the most crucial moments. The quality of the results produced was no more and no less than the clarity of my thoughts and the quality of my communication.

And if I were to judge the effectiveness of my leadership based on the significance of the results produced, then I can easily correlate the most important results with the quality of the relationship I had with my team. I can play back the tapes in my mind and see and hear myself in conversations when people on my team freely joined me and gave their very best to produce the outcomes we had promised.

Yes, Timmy, we adults can create situations when work can be boring, even exhausting. But when we are relating and communicating, it is exhilarating!

Your Leadership Legacy?

Occasionally, I will add a little trail running in the desert to my regular workouts as a change of pace. Invariably, I pass people on the trail sharing a recent conversation—"So I said...; then he says...; so I'm like all...; and he goes...." The person being discussed is always characterized by a replaying of an entire conversation in a dramatically exaggerated manner. Think about it. Who do you remember? Aren't many of your most emotionally poignant memories somehow linked to conversations, the things that were said or not said?

When it's all said and done, what will you be remembered for as a leader? What will be the lasting impact you made on the people you led? How will their values, ethics, commitment and personal vision have changed as result of your leadership? What conversations will they remember, and what stories will be told about your leadership? It is said that a culture is best represented by the stories told about the organization. The measure of your leadership may be the stories people tell about you after you've gone.

We are remembered for what we say (or don't say) and for how it was said. How are your conversations being replayed? Are you characterized as uplifting and motivating? Visionary? Wise? Vulnerable and open? Honest? Strong? Accessible? Your legacy is being created with every word you speak.

CHAPTER EIGHTEEN

In which we learn how to never be without an answer, even to our greatest dilemmas, if we'll just listen and follow the simple directions.

A SURPRISING SOURCE OF GUIDANCE

It's amazing how people can surprise you. Just when you think you know them, something shocking is revealed.

Not long ago I was sitting on the patio, having a cup of coffee and enjoying a beautiful morning in Tucson, Arizona, with Molly, a beautiful 82-year-old woman I love and admire. Not only was the day gorgeous, but so was this remarkable woman.

She had such vitality and zest that I felt energized just being near her, listening to her tell me about hiking the Grand Canyon, rim to rim, several years earlier when she was 78 years old. Seventy-eight years old, and hiking the Grand Canyon? Yes, and so much more. It wasn't unusual for her to start the day with a 30-mile bike ride, play tennis and end the day with a moonlight hike.

One would never guess Molly was in pain that morning. A year earlier, she had crashed her bike on a trail in Vail, Colorado, breaking her back and several ribs. She could handle the pain. It was how the injuries had slowed her down a bit and had triggered a nervous leg syndrome that frustrated her the most. Only those closest to her knew how she suffered.

As Molly and I talked that morning, our conversation turned to a topic we had shared before. It seemed to us that most people are challenged at least once (and often more than once) by a major disruption in their life. We both knew people who had used the disruption to powerfully move their lives forward while others were immobilized by their thoughts of having to relive a potential disaster in the future.

We talked about our own life experiences when we each had been the most frightened—facing either what seemed like our own death or the imminent loss of a loved one. In those moments, we had both noticed that we had been guided by an unseen presence, one that was calming and assuring. One that knew exactly what to do if we just listened.

I told her about a battlefield experience when I had felt a reassuring hand on my shoulder. The pressure of the hand was telling me to keep my head down for just another minute. Thinking it was my sergeant, I reached back to put my hand over his to let him know I was okay, but I felt nothing but my own shoulder. No one was near me, yet somehow I knew immediately I would find a way out and survive. I had been restored by an invisible touch.

Molly then said something I will never forget.

In a matter of fact way she said, "…like the time I was attacked and almost raped." I couldn't believe and didn't want to accept what I was hearing. I interrupted her and asked what she was talking about. She said, "You know. It was the time that man broke into the house."

She disclosed to me how it happened in the mid 1950s at the peak of the Cold War, when her husband served in the Strategic Air Command. His mission was to fly over the North Pole and bomb Moscow if Russia attacked the U.S. At least once a month his crew was put on "alert" where they spent the week in a concrete bunker only a few yards away from a fully fueled B52 bomber armed with nuclear weapons.

One night when her husband was away on a mission, she went to a neighbor's house to play cards with her bridge club. Returning home at about 10 o'clock, she checked on her four children who were asleep in their bedrooms upstairs and then got ready for bed in the downstairs master bedroom. Living on the Air Force base, she felt safe and typically left the windows open and the doors unlocked. She fell asleep reading with the light on. The sound of her bedroom door opening startled her out of her slumber.

Standing in the doorway was a young soldier in uniform. He had a butcher knife from the kitchen in his hand. Paralyzed with fear, she barely managed to utter, "You better leave…you'll get in trouble." Ignoring what she said, the man held the knife to her throat and started to assault her. She suddenly thought of her children upstairs. What if they heard something and came into the room?

Looking straight into to his eyes, she said, "Stop it! If my children come down they will be frightened!" She immediately noticed a change in his eyes. She seized that moment and shouted, "What would your mother say if she saw you now!?"

Her words had more power than any weapon she could have used. The man got up saying, "I'm sorry. I didn't know you were a nice woman." She followed him out of the house through the kitchen door where he had come in and slammed it shut as he silently slunk away.

To this day, she still does not know where those powerful words came from. She wasn't trying to think of something clever to say or do. The thinking part of her brain had stepped aside to let a larger consciousness take over. She knows the trigger to those words was in his eyes. She couldn't have seen the answer if she had been trying to "think" her way out it. Fear was fueling her higher level of consciousness.

Like all of our emotions, fear can be employed as a wonderful asset. Gavin de Becker, author of *The Gift of Fear*, writes about a woman, who, like Molly, intuited something about her attacker that saved her life. Waving a gun, the attacker had commanded her not to move while he went into the kitchen. Yet the instant the attacker left the room, she stood up and followed him out the room. "I was literally right behind him, like a ghost, and he didn't know I was there. We walked down the hall together… When he moved on toward the kitchen, I turned and walked out through the living room."

De Becker tells us that it was fear that gave her the courage to get up and follow her attacker: "She later described a fear so complete that it replaced every feeling in her body…What she experienced was real fear, not when we are startled, not like the fear we feel at a movie, or the fear of public speaking. This is a powerful ally that says, 'Do what I tell you to do.' Sometimes it tells a person to play dead, or to stop breathing, or run or scream or fight."

In life-threatening situations, it's easy to operate on pure emotion. We don't really have a choice, but what about in everyday life? Most of us have been told from childhood to ignore those scary feelings. Business leaders have been trained to dismiss things like intuition and gut instinct. Emotions are a sign of weakness. Feelings get in the way of tough decisions. In fact, major or strategic decisions made intuitively and without rigorous analysis often lead to disastrous results, right?

Maybe.

Most scientific studies of how good business decisions are made tend to dismiss intuition or hunches. The only decision-making models that seem to stand up under scientific scrutiny are ones in which these steps are followed:

- Diagnose the symptoms and identify a root cause for the problem
- Generate a number of well-thought-out and/or "out-of-the box" options for correcting the problem
- Establish and rank the criteria for evaluating the options (cost, time to implement, how it affects various stake-holders, etc.)
- Evaluate each option against the selected criteria
- Select the best option and implement it

Yet when firefighters, pilots and combat soldiers are asked how they make decisions, they often say they didn't consider any options, they just acted. Of course, the results aren't always what they had intended, but then, neither are the results coming from the most thoroughly explored options. Besides, how do we really know when we have fully analyzed the options or even know if we are analyzing the right options? What tells you to stop analyzing and decide? In the end, I'll bet it's a feeling.

Even General George Patton, who did more "thinking" about the strategies of war than anyone, said, "A good plan, violently executed now, is better than a perfect plan next week." Patton also said, "A good solution applied with vigor now is better than a perfect solution applied ten minutes later."

In *Descartes' Error: Reason, Emotion and the Human Brain,* neurobiologist Antonio Damasio (1994) provides a case study of a brilliant attorney identified only as EVR who underwent brain surgery to have a tumor removed. It sheds some light on the significance of our emotions in decision-making. EVR not only survived the operation but his tremendous cognitive abilities were also left intact. His IQ still tested in the 99th percentile. Yet he became totally inept. He lost his job and couldn't keep a job after that. He squandered his savings, lost his house and his wife left him. EVR eventually went to Dr. Damasio for help.

Dr. Damasio tested EVR and all the results seemed to be within normal ranges. The doctor was baffled. But then a breakthrough occurred. When he asked EVR when he would like to schedule his next appointment, EVR couldn't decide. He could discuss the pros and cons of every possible date, but he couldn't make a choice.

This indecisiveness had become common for EVR. It took him hours to decide where to dine. He could rationally evaluate each restaurant's menu, seating arrangements, atmosphere and even its management. But he couldn't decide which one to choose. Further tests revealed that the surgery had disconnected the emotional center of his brain, the amygdala, from its prefrontal lobes. EVR had no feelings!

Damasio discovered that we do not make decisions like a computer. Our brain delivers answers to us in an emotional context we call a hunch, gut instinct or intuition. We feel a certain rightness or wrongness about our decisions. That sense is coming from the amygdala, the part of our brain that records all the feelings we experience throughout our lifetime and associates those feelings with the events (thoughts) that caused them.

Combining those stored emotions with the memory of decisions we've made or actions we've taken gives us an amazing ability for prediction. We can clump certain events, actions and circumstances together into familiar patterns and predict the future. We can detect imminent danger, liars, frauds and cheats. We can sense opportunity and right action. It's not mystically or divinely derived. It's called intuition. It's a source of wisdom that should not be ignored just because it is felt or sensed rather than analyzed.

Fortunately, Molly paid attention and saw something in the eyes of her attacker that saved her. It happened in a split second. Under normal circumstances she would have missed it. But her fear opened the door to pure magic. Her immediate transition from combative danger to safety came from a deeper place than logical thought has access to. It is very hard to logically think your way to your next transition. Transitions come from a deeper place than thought.

Daniel Goleman, a leading expert on Emotional Intelligence, describes it as "stealing resources from other parts of the brain to keep the senses hyper alert—a mental stance tailored to survival."

Molly had four very young children of her own and knew them well. They couldn't hide anything from her. Their faces portrayed everything—fear, anxiety, distress, sadness anger—and she saw those faces every day. Without knowing it, the loving attention she gave her children had made her masterful in sensing vulnerability.

When she yelled at the attacker to stop because of what she feared her children might be exposed to, Molly saw that something had signaled a shift in her attacker's mind. Who knows where his mind traveled in that moment? Perhaps to an image of his own mother or to an event in his childhood. It doesn't matter. Wherever his thoughts had gone and whatever he was thinking was cast in his facial expression and in his eyes, and only for an instant.

But Molly saw that change. She saw it as vulnerability and acted instantly. That is truly a gift. And by now you have probably intuited something. Yes, that's right. Molly is my mother. And that is truly a gift for me.

Honoring Your Gifts

In common or familiar situations, when are you unable to decide? Is it that you can't figure out what to do, or that you just don't like your alternatives? When I am clear, I notice that the first thought that comes to mind is ultimately the right course of action.

I can't prove it, but my experience strongly suggests that I usually know exactly what to do from the very beginning. But I may resist doing it because there is a part of me—head, heart, or gut—registering discomfort.

In our mind, we might hear something like "Call her," but then think, "No, she'll hang up." We hear "Apologize," but then think, "No, that's weak." We are getting clear guidance, but we rationalize a way to resist or avoid it. Whenever I make a decision based on resistance or avoidance, then I know I am not honoring my intuitive gifts. I am either believing a thought that is not true (such as "that's weak" or "I'll be rejected"), or I am betraying what I truly believe is the right action for the sake of expediency or comfort.

The strength of your intuition is easy enough to test. Whenever you need to make a tough decision, write down the first thought that comes to mind. Then go through whatever decision-making process you normally use. When the results are known, compare which decision would have produced the best outcome—your intuition or your formal decision-making process. The post mortem will help you either validate your intuition or help fine-tune it by discovering false beliefs, denial and rationalization.

CHAPTER NINETEEN

In which we learn how to delete all regret, shame and negative self-concepts by seeing them as beliefs that are in conflict with reality.

FINDING THE GIFT INSIDE THE TRUTH

My mother, Molly, saved herself using a gift called face reading. Most of us can face-read to some extent. We react almost automatically to the changing expressions displayed on another's face. A smile, a frown, a lifted brow or even a blink creates an impression of what another person is thinking or feeling.

When my daughter Jenny was thirteen, her ability to roll her eyes expressed more annoyance at her "dumb old Dad" than words alone…although there were many more words exchanged after those episodes than she had bargained for!

I have to confess that I love watching faces. When I'm standing in line at the coffee shop or at the grocery store, I watch the cashiers' faces. The range of emotions I witness expressed through "face language' is quite remarkable. In five or six transactions, I see happiness, fear, anger, annoyance, impatience, indifference, and kindness. Not only do I see it, but also I feel it through my own reactions to the scene playing out in front of me.

When I'm coaching, I'm also noticing my reactions to what is being signaled by my client's face. In a session, I am totally focused on my client. It's as if I am with the only other person in the world. I listen intently. And the more intently I listen, the more visually focused I become. One sense amplifies the other. Without really being conscious of it, I am face reading. I am interpreting at a deep level what I'm seeing as much as what I'm hearing.

That is why I remind my clients that I will often interrupt them and ask a question. Something I hear or see will spark an intuitive insight. Rather than let the moment pass, I blurt it out. I will say something or ask a question that some clients might experience as "reading their minds." But I am only reacting to the barrage of signals. And I'm not always right. It isn't an exact science, but I've learned when to trust my intuition and when to ignore it.

There is an especially delightful expression I love to witness when I coach. It flashes across a client's face for less than a second as they discover a truth about themselves that they've refused to acknowledge for years. I call it a "gleek."

It's the look of a kid caught with his hand in the cookie jar. It usually happens as a client is justifying why they are the way they are. When they hear the absurd, self-limiting belief spoken out loud for the first time, they immediately know it's not true. That's the moment they gleek.

But rather than stop their artfully constructed story, they often just go on with it. They have a lot invested in the belief. It's hard to let go. The thought has served them well a thousand different times. It helps create their logical, well-thought-out excuses, rationalizations, judgments and justifications. All the roadblocks to transition. But the gleek is my signal to interrupt and ask, "Is that true?"

Many clients initially defend their belief. They have been collecting evidence for years, creating an airtight case that they are somehow limited or at an unnatural disadvantage. Is it true? Can you be sure it's true? Asked at the right time, the question can create powerful insight and a joyous sense of freedom and release. Why? Because deep down and in their hearts, they know it's not true. It's that discovery and personal insight I most love to share with my clients.

Phil, a businessman in his late forties, had a wonderful wide-eyed gleek. We had met at a business conference a year earlier and had stayed in touch, meeting for breakfast when he came to Phoenix on business. The first-born son to a Greek immigrant family living in New York, Phil had been driven all his life to succeed. To him that meant nothing less than winning and being the best. As a kid growing up in an ethnic neighborhood he was a scrappy fighter and a fierce competitor. His athletic skills led to playing professional baseball right out of high school, but an injury in his first year abruptly ended his baseball career.

Keeping his promise to his mother to get a college degree, Phil worked his way through business school and graduated with honors in accounting. It didn't take long before a well-known Fortune 500 company in the consumer products industry recruited him. Seen as a high-potential and talented young executive, Phil was promoted early and often. His success continued even in an environment of ongoing mergers, reorganizations and transfers.

There was a problem, though. In fifteen years, he and his wife had moved at least 10 different times. They wanted to settle down before their kids started junior high school, and Phil resigned shortly afterwards.

Phil and his family loved the West, skiing in Colorado and enjoying the beaches of California during their vacations. They decided to move to San Diego where Phil planned to consult and eventually buy or start a business. That was five years ago, and Phil still had not started or bought a business. He had looked at dozens of opportunities but nothing seemed to be a good fit. When I first met him, he was still consulting.

At breakfast one morning, Phil said, "Jim, there's a reason I wanted to meet you today. I haven't been honest with you. You see, my consulting practice has never really amounted to much at all. I'm reaching a point where I have to make a change. I've never earned enough in consulting fees to cover my living expenses, so I've been tapping into my savings for years now. All that hard earned equity I'd socked away from my corporate years is shrinking every month. If I hadn't been so lucky in a couple of real estate deals, I'd be broke now. I never thought I'd hear myself say that."

He went on, "I've never failed before. I feel terrible. Some mornings I don't want to get out of bed. When I do finally get up, I go to a coffee shop, read the paper, and surf the internet...you know, doing market research and such. But none of the leads are panning out for me. I'm really feeling stuck, Jim. Nothing's going right for me. I'm slowly going broke, and I don't know what to do."

I smiled and asked, "Phil, you don't know what to do? You're going to end up destitute and homeless because you don't know what to do? You just don't know what to do. Is that true?" I let it hang there while he searched my face to see if I was insulting him or sincerely challenging his thinking.

That's when he gleeked.

After a while, he started laughing. "Oh, brother! That was really pathetic, wasn't it? I can't believe I said that. I know exactly what to do. I want to go back to work and make a difference. I've never truly enjoyed consulting. I've wanted to for more than a year, but I thought if I gave up on consulting, it would be selling out. Only losers quit, right? Damn! It's so simple. I'm going to get a job!"

It can happen that quickly. When a client confronts the lies they've been telling themselves, it can create an immediate release. A belief is challenged, found to be false and the world changes. Just like that.

But something else equally powerful can happen. It's the realization that we do some pretty bizarre things to cover up those beliefs—beliefs such as: I'm stupid, or unattractive, or inept and a fraud. What does a person trying not to be judged as stupid do to cover it up? They nod like a bobble-head doll and repeat "hmmm, very interesting" over and over, fearing to offer an original thought...or ask an innocent question and appear "stupid."

The repeated behavior is often referred to as a "routine." Just like a stand-up comic's act, their routine starts to distinguish them. Like the routine of using anger to regain control of a scary situation: "Oh, there she goes again, she really blew up and let that poor guy have it when he criticized her department." And ironically, the routine inadvertently creates the very impression we most feared, that we are immature, stupid or afraid.

I know about these routines. I've had my own. When I was younger and felt intimidated, I would become very terse and attempt a scowl that I had learned watching my Dad when he was angry. It was my quiet, tough guy act. I remember my first day on the job with Johnson and Johnson at one of their large manufacturing and distribution centers. I was scared. I had no business experience at all, and my job was to manage the distribution center. I was in my early twenties and at the height of my perfectionism. What I feared most was looking foolish or inept.

The distribution center was 250,000 square feet stocked with every product J&J produced—pharmaceuticals, hospital packs, athletic tape, floss, and baby shampoo. Boxes stacked forty feet high, fork lifts everywhere, and 20 dock doors with trucks ready to be loaded. I didn't even know the difference between UPS and USPS. It would be just a matter of time before I was exposed.

Besides that, I was already looking pretty foolish. During my graduation party a week earlier, things had gotten out of hand. I have to admit to having one beer too many, and I managed to put my face in front of a friend's fist late that night. The impact split my forehead open just above the bridge of my nose, leaving two gaping inch-long vertical cuts at the beginning of each eyebrow. I didn't get the cuts medically treated or stitched, so the scabs that formed looked like little horns sprouting out of my forehead. How was I going to explain that?

Maybe no one would notice. No such luck. As soon as I walked into the plant, the receptionist said, "Wow, what happened? That must have hurt!"

"Yeah, rugby. Playing rugby, and, well, you know, it's a pretty rough game."

Rugby! Why did I say that? I could have said anything, like the truth for instance, but I tried to lie my way out of it. I didn't know anything about rugby except that I had watched a few practices, and the rugby team looked tougher than hockey players. I prayed no one would ask me what position I played or anything about the game. My tough guy routine was under way.

I thought I needed to hide my discomfort. I thought if I looked and acted tough, no one would see how afraid I was. And it was a logical way of explaining my horns without going into the story about "one beer too many." Fortunately, my manager didn't buy the tough guy act. I think he must have seen the nervous fear written on my face, and he gently let me off the hook. I've never forgotten what he said to me that morning as he walked me around the plant.

"Jim, you can't hurt this company. You can't possibly make enough mistakes to create any lasting harm to J&J. There's nothing to fear. I want you to treat this just like it's your own little candy store. You own it, and you manage it." That was my orientation. He walked away, and my world changed. Just like that.

The Ostrich Syndrome

How ironic it is that what we don't want others to know about us is so readily apparent. We try to bury one aspect of our self-concept, and other aspects are exaggerated to compensate. There are parts of us falsely inflated to shield the part we don't want seen. The problem, of course, is that the shield is somewhat transparent. After a while, someone is going to see through that shield. Like an ostrich hiding its tiny head in the sand with its big rear-end in full view, we can act like, well, like big rear-ends when we try to hide our tiny fear or shame.

Even more ironic is that when fully examined in the light of day, we find that our darkest secrets are not true at all. I am stupid. I ruined my life. I was taken advantage of because I wasn't strong enough. I am a failure. I am not good enough. Is it true? Or could it be a convenient alibi for refusing the call to be who you truly are?

CHAPTER TWENTY

In which we learn how to use our mind and body to ground our emotions and reclaim our spirit.

LEARNING HOW TO TRANSITION IN THE MOMENT

Anthony is gone. He was here a few seconds ago, and now he's gone. Anthony is time traveling again.

Of course, he doesn't physically vanish. His body is still in front of me where he left it. But everything else that defines him is gone. He is staring directly at me but doesn't see me. His face is expressionless, almost as if he's in a coma. His mind is traveling to an event that happened in the past. I don't say anything while he is away. I know he'll be back in a few seconds.

It doesn't take a whole lot of skill to read a face and know that it's time traveling. Even my dog, Koda, can do it. He's a Yellow Lab and loves to retrieve. Twice a day we'll go out for a few minutes and he runs and fetches a thickly knotted piece of rope, about 14 inches long, his favorite toy. If he follows all my commands and runs at full pace, I'll tug and pull on the rope with him as a reward. An old piece of rope and fifteen seconds of tug-of-war, and Koda is in dog heaven.

A short time ago, I was in the back yard, playing fetch with Koda. During the first few seconds of tugging on the rope, I drifted off to an earlier conversation I had that morning with a client. I was time traveling. I was daydreaming. When I came back a few seconds later, I noticed that Koda had stopped tugging and was watching my face waiting for me to be present again. Living beings all know when someone has left them.

I don't know how it is for you, but when I am with a person who is lost in their thoughts, I experience it as the person actually being gone. To me they are out of their body and not present.

When I am fully present, I feel most alive. Everything is acting in concert—mind, body, heart and spirit. I am here. I can feel my heart beat. I can feel the sensation of energy flowing into my core as I draw in a breath. I see, hear and feel. I notice that my only emotion is one of gratitude. I love being alive.

Until I start to think again. And when I do, I slip away and go to another place, just like my new client, Anthony, did when he pulled his disappearing act.

Anthony is the new CEO of a large, metropolitan for-profit healthcare system with four hospitals. He is operating under a great deal of stress. His job is to turn around an organization with a history of financial shortfalls. Those shortfalls were the reasons the last CEO and CFO were fired. The board wanted him to make quick work of it. Fortunately, Anthony's first several months on the job looked brilliant with every key performance indicator moving in the right direction.

When I walked into his office a few minutes earlier, he had been nervously shuffling papers and restacking the file folders on his desk. He said hello without looking up and pointed to an empty chair in front of his desk. Still not making eye contact, he asked me, "What's new and exciting?" It was his standard greeting.

Sensing his distraction, I didn't answer and sat down while he finished organizing his desk. He didn't seem to notice that I hadn't answered his question. There was a slight tremor in his hands. I gave him time to settle his thoughts. When he finally looked up, I asked, "How are you feeling, right now?"

Anthony responded with the standard "Fine. Yeah, thanks. I'm okay."

"Let me try again, Anthony. I wasn't making small talk. I wanted to know how you are feeling, right now in this moment." Still talking in executive code, he said he was feeling a little tense and had an extreme sense of urgency.

Sense of urgency? That wasn't urgency he was feeling. That was pure anxiety. But I didn't press the point. I remembered my own helplessness as an executive who ignored what my body was trying to tell me.

He went on and told me about a conversation he had with his controller earlier that week. There was an impending $2 million "surprise" that had to be written off this quarter. It had been improperly accounted for last year under the former management, but the problem was now Anthony's. The board of directors demanded that he dramatically reduce expenses while increasing billings as much as possible in the upcoming quarter to make up for the unexpected loss.

When I asked a clarifying question, I noticed he had checked out on me. He was gone. I could see the vacancy in his eyes. When I saw that he was back in the present, I asked where he went.

He had drifted back to an earlier teleconference with his board when he notified them about the loss. He thought about what he should have said but didn't say. He worried what they must be thinking about him. His mind also had traveled to a looming catastrophe he was creating about the future.

He dreaded telling his senior management team that despite their progress, they would have to cut expenses again. It was already tough enough. This just might push several of his most competent managers to start looking elsewhere. His mind moved continuously from the past and into the future and back again, seldom staying in the present moment.

As he spoke, his voice had that telltale waver caused by the excess adrenaline pumping through his body. His breathing was shallow, like he was having an asthma attack.

"Look, Anthony, I'd like to drop the agenda we created for today. I know how much you care and how committed you are to achieving the goals we've created for your professional development, but if something doesn't change, the two hours we spend together each week will not produce the results you signed up for. The coaching we do over the next six months will be a waste...unless you are willing to learn to coach yourself and manage your own mental, physical and emotional states."

Anthony said nothing.

So I pulled my chair closer and told Anthony how for years I had operated from the mistaken notion that I was at my best when fueled by high levels of stress hormones. I think that men are especially misled by things like locker room scenes of players banging their heads against their locker doors to stoke themselves into a competitive fury. It's as if we need anger to cover our fear of taking appropriate action.

The problem with that is that it cuts off the thinking parts of our brain. The more stress we're under, the more our brain functions switch to the emergency centers of the brain. We react more than think. It's fight or flight.

I finished by saying, "With the extreme amount of stress you are creating right now, you are probably operating at a very primitive level."

I shared with Anthony how I had learned that I was actually far more effective and even more powerful when I was calm yet energized, relaxed but fully under control. I could access all my faculties—thinking, feeling, sensing and moving.

Think of times when the stakes are high and there are no clear answers. A decision has to be made quickly. In these tough situations, I find that I am most confident when my head, heart, gut and the seat of my pants are in full accord—whole body alignment.

Have you ever made a decision and had a nagging sense that it wouldn't work out? I have, and those decisions proved to be my worst. On the other hand, when everything—head, heart, gut and the seat of my pants—is aligned, I have made some of my best decisions ever.

- **Head**

  Think! Consider the full range of options and their implications. See! Look at the situation as it really exists. Don't window-dress it or make it any worse than it is. Hear! Talk it over and listen. Ask questions of experts, advisors and trusted insiders.

- **Heart**
  How does it feel? Are you acting in alignment with your values? Is your integrity "in" or is it "out"? Check your emotions. Are you happy, sad, anxious, or afraid?

- **Gut**
  We can be highly instinctive or sensing. We have learned and internalized a lot about being alive. We are constantly taking in information, assessing it, contrasting it, and translating it. We are picking up patterns and other subtle indicators that escape the conscious eye, but our internal systems are processing the information. For me, gut instinct is the language of the mind and body. It tells us when something is right or when something's wrong.

- **Seat of the Pants**
  What is happening now? Has something shifted or changed? Am I on solid ground? If you have an opportunity, check out the seat in a racecar or a fighter jet. Notice that there is no, or very little, padding. When you are buckled in, you become a part of the machine. The pilot or driver can detect the slightest change in the performance characteristics, changes that might not even show up in the instrumentation.

People get in trouble when they either overuse a particular body center or block one or two centers with stress. We all have a center that we tend to use more than the others. For example, some people rely solely on logic while others are constantly tuned into their feelings. But we operate at our highest levels of consciousness by bringing all the centers into alignment.

The only natural method I know for achieving that peak whole-body state of consciousness is learning how to relax and reduce stress levels on demand. I told Anthony about some of those practices.

"There is a practice I'd like you to do every day for at least two weeks. There are two parts to it—one helps you see how your thinking affects your body while the other helps you unwind the effects on your body. Many people who use this simple practice over an extended period of time find that they can change their emotional and mental states and move into a peak performance zone on demand. The practice takes about 30 minutes a day. Do you want to hear more?"

He said that he was willing to listen.

"Okay, good. First take a deep breath, pause, and slowly exhale. Did you feel a sense of release when you exhaled? Not everyone does. Try it again."

Anthony took several breaths and said, "Yes, I think I know what you mean. I can feel a slight reduction of the tension in my chest."

"Great. Most people, but not everyone, experience a sense of reduced tension or feel a release when they exhale. What do you feel when you inhale? Just breathe for about 30 seconds and follow your breath. Use your diaphragm and breathe into your belly. In and out. Naturally." I timed him for about half a minute.

Anthony said, "Jim, I'm not sure what I'm supposed to feel, but it doesn't feel like the air is filling my lungs. It seems to flow right here," he said pointing at his belly, midway between his sternum and his navel.

"That's right. I experience it as energy flowing into my body." I asked him to try it again, but this time, without added effort, to imagine the flow moving a little lower to a place in his core just behind his naval.

He nodded his head as he experienced the sensation of his breath being drawn into his body and the release of tension and discomfort as he exhaled. He could feel the sensation of energy as it flowed through his body.

What I was telling Anthony is one of the most effective ways for people to be present; that is, to have an awareness in the here and now. It is a vital practice that can enhance your self-awareness and self-regulation. As I said before, you can't transition to higher states without first grounding yourself in present moment reality.

It has been demonstrated that many people who regularly practice the breathing technique for 15 minutes twice a day, can learn to control their level of stress, bringing it back down from high anxiety into the peak performance range just by breathing. It has also been shown that we can just as easily increase our positive stress level from a drowsy or sleepy state back to the peak performance range with active movement. For example, try raising your arms over your head, lifting your face up toward the sky, and smiling the biggest, goofiest smile you've ever smiled. It's an instantaneous transition.

I said to Anthony, "Let's see if we can find the source of your distraction. This is the second part of the practice. I'm inviting you to keep a detailed log of your day from the time you arise until you go to bed during the next 10 days. You can use a daily calendar, but capture as much detail as possible—just like your attorney does but in 30-minute increments. Have your assistant help by reminding you at least once an hour—email, sticky-note, or tap on the door, whatever is comfortable for both of you.

I continued and requested, "Note what are you doing and what you are accomplishing. I am especially interested in your assessment of the value of your activity. After each entry, note the level of stress you feel, using a scale from 1 to 10, whether you enjoy doing it, dislike doing it or have a neutral feeling about it.

"If your stress level is below 3 or higher than 6, please note what you were thinking at the time. If you were at a level one and felt tired and drowsy, you may have been avoiding something. If you are at a level 5 or higher, notice if you stopped listening or started daydreaming—plus any discomfort in your body, especially your back, neck chest, or stomach. If you can, capture any one-liners you were thinking, like the one we talked about last week. Remember? You said, 'There's no accountability around here. Everyone is passing the buck!'" Anthony was very detail oriented and said he would start the journal the next morning.

I recommended he purchase a progressive relaxation tape and practice the skill for 15 to 30 minutes a day. I enjoy the *Guided Body Scan* by Jon Kabat-Zinn, Ph.D., and *Relaxation Systems* by Dr. Jeffery Thompson. Many executives find *Calm Amid Crisis— An Executive Guide to Reducing Stress through Meditation* by Charles Graybar an excellent resource. Aaron Hemsley has also produced a number of exceptional audiocassette programs for maximizing performance. I've found that these practices help me maintain a state of mind that produces high energy and full engagement every day, no matter what comes at me or what the challenge is.

In our sessions that followed, I helped Anthony question the stressful thoughts he experienced using a form of inquiry developed by Byron Katie (www.thework.com). Were they true? Could he absolutely know they were true? How had he reacted when he believed they were true? Who would he be without the thought? This method of inquiry is among the most simple yet most powerful forms of inquiry I have found—especially for self-coaching. I use it myself every day.

After only a few days of making entries in his journal, Anthony called me seeking assurance that he was interpreting his stress levels correctly. "Jim, I'm noticing that I seldom experience anything less than a level 5 during the day. I wake up and go to bed feeling stress. I can handle it okay, and it's never reached level 8. But I seem to be running at a level 5, 6, or 7 all day. If I'm not experiencing stress, then I just feel exhausted. I'm tired, and worn out."

It's not an unusual situation. I've worked with many executives trapped in crisis mode, usually one of their own making. It's a red flag warning. My experience has been that what follows the complaints of stress and crisis by the leader is more complaints about their team. "I can't trust them. No one is accountable. They just don't have the critical skills they need to get the job done." Anthony was no different. It didn't take him long before he started blaming his team for his problems. I suggested that we meet as soon as possible and take a look at his journal entries.

As we reviewed his journal several days later, Anthony tended to express a lot of remorse over events that he handled poorly. I helped him connect with what he was thinking at the time and how that affected his behavior. He discovered a pattern of distrust and blame, even when he had only the flimsiest scrap of circumstantial evidence that someone had let him down. He recognized how his fear of looking bad had him seek out scapegoats wherever he could find them.

I'd seen the cycle before. The boss, under stress, gives confused, indirect and incomplete direction to the team. When the team responds in a confused manner, the boss leaps to a conclusion that the team is incompetent. Fearing the worst, the boss takes on the most critical work herself. The team sees that they are not trusted or valued, and they feel a lower sense of commitment. The boss in turn sees this as proof that the team is incompetent and unreliable. And so it goes, from bad to worse.

Anthony recognized that in emotionally pitched situations he used anger as a way to manipulate people with his emotional outbursts. Whenever Anthony was feeling anxious or uncomfortable, he would explode and shut down the conversation. It was an easy way for him to escape the issue and transfer his stress to his subordinates.

I helped him reconstruct the conversations that had not produced the outcome he had intended. He learned to replay those awkward events in his mind but in the replay seeing himself act with poise and grace, in an image of his ideal self. We would role-play the most challenging situations until we were both satisfied with his progress. Without really understanding how it was occurring, Anthony was rewiring his brain and training his mind by envisioning an ideal self.

In less than a month, he started catching himself in the act. Anthony explained it as an out-of-body experience where he could see himself starting to lose control, but not quite in time. Later, he learned to catch it in the moment, compose himself and then go on. After several months, situations that used to threaten him and result in an emotional outburst tended to occur less frequently. After six months, the old triggers didn't exist. Anthony had learned to coach himself.

Transitioning in the Moment

For many years, it was believed that our brains are 'hard-wired." In other words, there wasn't a lot of evidence to refute popular excuses like "I was born that way. It's just the way I am, and there's nothing I can do about it!"

Furthermore, because our mind is capable of generating about 50,000 to 60,000 thoughts a day, those thoughts actually do create deep-seated neural pathways and powerful habits of mind. But we are learning more about the plasticity of the brain. We have discovered that we do have the ability to literally change "the way we are."

Leading researchers like Dr. Daniel Goleman, a noted psychologist in the field of emotional intelligence, and neurologist Dr. Richard Restak along with many other scientists are reporting the amazing ability we have to literally rewire our brains. Dr. Restak in his book The New Brain: How The Modern Age Is Rewiring Your Mind *reports that "we now know that the brain never loses the power to transform itself on the basis of experience, and this transformation can occur over very short intervals." So do you let random experiences like newscasts and false interpretations of briefly observed events transform your brain, or do you take responsibility for changing the way you think and experience the world?*

Here's the good news. By using the simple awareness exercises outlined in this chapter and the inquiry approach developed by Byron Katie, found at www.thework.com, you can transform the way you experience the world. And you can easily maintain your transformation with a regular practice of meditation, inquiry and awareness; however, I do have a warning. It is my experience that without a daily practice, the mind will atrophy and revert to old habits within a matter of days. It atrophies ten times faster than an unexercised muscle. But exercise your mind daily and you will develop an extraordinary ability to transition instantaneously, on demand.

CHAPTER TWENTY-ONE

*In which we learn to make our most powerful transitions—
not by escaping from the past or controlling the future—
but by becoming what we are.*

WHAT CAN BE LEARNED FROM SILENCE

The story I'm about to tell is true. It occurred near the end of the writing of this book when someone I trusted completely suggested I do an exercise which would once again take me into the gap, where I could question my most deeply held beliefs. And it happened exactly this way. To relive it, I'll narrate it in the present tense to reflect my state of mind that day:

A man walks through the streets of Los Angeles in silence. His pockets are empty, and he has no money or identification. He hasn't eaten for two days, but doesn't notice his hunger. His mind is at peace.

For more than a week he has learned to quiet his mind as he walks, and with conscious effort thinks only in the most primitive terms. He names everything he sees but limits the name to a single noun—man, tree, car, woman, concrete. He holds no concepts about what he sees. He doesn't drift into events from the past or worry about the future. If a concept or story appears, he releases it before it can take hold of his mind.

Wearing an old blue tee shirt and crumpled pair of khakis, he looks deeply into the eyes of those he passes by. Few people meet his gaze, and the few who do quickly avert their eyes. His mind is quiet about that. He understands.

He has no idea where he is going or why he keeps walking. At each intersection he pauses and waits for it to be decided. Straight ahead, left, right or sit down? He does not backtrack, walking only in a direction that takes him to a place he has not yet seen. Right. Left. Straight. Straight. Right. Left. Straight. The man walks without purpose but not aimlessly. He understands he is being carried away from the mainstream, away from the streets crowded with traffic, tourists, skaters and latte drinkers.

A woman walks toward him wearing a vintage military trench coat and helmet. She is a person of color—her skin is dark chocolate brown, but her face is painted white. Her lips are bright red. She looks deeply into his eyes and asks a question.

"Do you listen to www.glennmiller.com?"

He looks back at her warmly but without speaking. She notices that she is not getting an answer, and she abruptly turns away and moves on. And so does he.

He walks under a bright afternoon sun. He feels his skin starting to burn and looks for a shady spot. In the distance he sees a small structure at the top of a knoll that overlooks a seaside park. It looks like a gazebo or small rotunda. It seems to be deserted, but as he nears the gazebo he sees the silhouettes of several people. Some are lying down asleep or passed out, others are slumped over holding their heads in their hands. Two men are passing a bottle in a paper bag. One woman sitting by herself watches them intently as they take long drinks from the bottle.

He enters the gazebo silently looking at each face before he sits down. Only the two men passing the bottle take notice. They meet his gaze and the older of the two says, "Welcome, stranger. Have a seat." He sits, saying nothing but keeping his eyes locked on theirs. He thinks only, "Man. Man. Sky. Grass. Ocean." He feels safe. His heart warms and is filled with gratitude.

Again the older man with the bottle says, "Can you talk? Do you understand me? Can you tell us who you are?" speaking gently, as if to a small child.

The silent man looks back at him feeling the caring nature of the questions, but does not answer. The older man hands the bottle to his friend and takes a few steps toward the silent man. "I was born here. Lived here all my life. This is my home. When I was a little boy, I would come here, and I sat right there, where you're sitting, and listened to the old Jewish men tell stories about the old country. Where do you come from?"

Getting no answer, the older man sits back down, looks back at the silent man, and takes a drink. His friend who had not taken his eyes off the silent man says, "I can read people by looking into their eyes." He points with the first two fingers of his left hand at his own eyes and then at the silent man's and back to his. "Look at him. He has Jesus in him. I can see it. There's a glow. Look."

The older man replies, "I don't know about Jesus, but he has God in him. That's for sure. He is a man of peace, isn't he?" The men continue talking in soft and reverent tones, sharing with each other how they experience the silent but peaceful man's presence. The silent man knows that the men are only expressing what lay deep in their own hearts. The God they were experiencing was the one they knew, the one in them. Still his heart is bursting, filling with love for these gentle people. Tears well in his eyes as the men continue to talk, "Yes, this is a good man. He understands. He knows what it's like to be here."

The woman who had been watching them suddenly stands up and says, "This is crazy. I'm leaving." The older man tells her, "Don't worry. You can stay. We won't hurt him. It's okay." She walks out looking back at the silent man with a fearful glance.

Taking another drink from the bottle, the older man gets up to take a closer look at the silent man. Keeping a respectful distance, the older man bends down putting his hands on his knees to steady himself as he stares intently at the silent man. Finally he asks, "Can you hear me? Do you speak English?" The silent man gives a slight nod in answer to his questions.

Just then another man hunched over and holding his gut, staggers into the gazebo. The silent man stands up. It feels crowded and no longer peaceful. The older man who is standing closest says, "He's all right. He won't hurt you, either."

The silent man smiles at this and starts to walk out of the gazebo. The older man grabs his arm. The other man stands up blocking the silent man's way out. The silent man turns to the one holding his arm and looks into his eyes. The older man says, "Please don't go," as he wraps his arms around the silent man embracing him like a long-lost son. He buries his face into the shoulder of the silent man. They stand holding each other, neither aware of time but each one knowing when it is complete.

The other man who is blocking the way says, "Excuse me. I just took a drink. My breath stinks. Is it okay...?" He tentatively puts his hand on the silent man's shoulder, kneels down a little and puts his face on the silent man's chest. The silent man holds him gently placing his hands on the back of the man's head. When the kneeling man releases him, the silent man walks out without looking back.

As he walks away, he releases the mental reins he had been holding back all day and lets his mind run free with what had just happened. He feels unsteady, his head swirls. His most deeply held beliefs about people, even what he believed about himself, begin to shatter. He realizes that what had seemed like a dream sequence just moments ago is reality. It was the rest of his life in which he had been sleepwalking. He looks for a place to sit alone.

Seeing a patch of grass in the deserted park below, he descends a concrete stairway. Halfway down he sees a man sitting on a step facing away toward the small park. The man on the stairway rests his extended left arm on a knee while he fumbles with something in his right hand. The silent man's mind is working freely now, and it creates a story that the sitting man could be dangerous if surprised. The silent man clears his throat and scrapes his shoes to alert the man below. The sitting man quickly pulls his arm in to his stomach and hunches over. The silent man steps around him and continues down the stairway. He stills his mind by thinking simply "Man. Grass. Tree. Ocean."

He walks to the tree and lies down on his back spread-eagled in the cool damp grass. Savoring the richness of what he had just experienced, he lets thoughts come freely again. He had said nothing in the gazebo. He didn't tell them who he was, what he did or what he had done in the past. He did not seek their approval or trust. He did not humble himself or ingratiate himself in any way. He had not attempted to be empathetic or feel their pain. He had done nothing, absolutely nothing, and he received what he had been seeking all his life...unconditional love. Nothing was given nor was anything expected in return.

No longer silent, the man starts to weep and then sobs uncontrollably. For the first time that he can remember, he had allowed someone to love him freely. He hadn't even allowed it. It just happened. Unconditional love. It was something he was unwilling to do for himself or let anyone else do. Not even his beautiful wife, children, or parents. He had come to believe that he had to be perfect to be loved. That he had made far too many mistakes, things he deeply regretted or was ashamed of, to deserve love.

He keeps thinking, "I did nothing. Absolutely nothing. But the men in the gazebo experienced something in me that had allowed them see the best of who they were. How can that be? Were they delusional? Am I?"

And then just as uncontrollably, he starts to laugh. He sees the delusion. He had always been perfect. The perfect him. No one else could be him. He was perfect for the job. He just couldn't see it. He had lived a false life of ambition and striving in order to earn the acceptance of others. The very thing he was unwilling to give himself. And he didn't have to do or accomplish or be anything at all. He could be nothing and that was perfect.

He wonders who those men were in the gazebo. He had a sense he had seen the older man before. Those eyes. There was something about his eyes. Had he looked into them before? Where was it? His mind suddenly reels with the image of the man he saw as a friend in the jungle so many years before. His mind jumps to the mirror he stared into that very morning as he looked into his own eyes. It had always been looking back at him. What he had feared, loved, or hated had been his own projected image. He had created the world in his own image. And finally in that gazebo, holding no image of himself, he was able to love unconditionally.

Discovering the Perfect You

I cannot say it any more eloquently than did Joseph Campbell:
"The privilege of a lifetime is being who you are."

Transitioning Beyond Coincidence

*"'It's a poor sort of memory that only works backwards,'
the Queen remarked."*
Through the Looking Glass by Lewis Carroll

It is several hours before sunrise, and I am sitting at my desk in our library. In a little more than an hour or so, the predawn light will crest the McDowell Mountains to the east and fill the morning air with violet and golden hues. I've seen the sun rise in many places, from Frankfurt to Saigon. Each has its own distinct aura, but none comes close to the colors of dawn in the Arizona desert. It's my favorite time of day.

My wife, Patsy, and I live in a small home built almost fifty years ago in an area that was once considered the outskirts of Phoenix. Designed for desert living, the house has a flat roof; and the exterior walls are made of stucco, common to what you might see in Santa Fe or Taos.

We love this old house. We're happy here and for now it feels like this is where we belong. A former owner remodeled it, installing large picture windows along the north side of the house. We chose a room with two of those large windows for the library. From my desk, I can look out across the desert landscape and watch the night become day. This is where I meditate, pray, write and read each morning.

I've sat here in this room and meditated about that afternoon with those gentle people in the gazebo. For me, few experiences are richer than discovering once again how little I know about what is true. I love having old beliefs shattered and superficial concepts peeled back for more truth to be uncovered. And on that day in the gazebo, I saw how an old self-concept had limited how I experienced love. Since that day I have come to see something else about love.

As I described that day in the last chapter, I made a distinction about love being unconditional. I perceived that it was given to me without condition, for being and doing nothing. What I have come to see is that love cannot be given nor can it be taken. Like an ocean, it cannot be owned, controlled, given or taken. Love just is. If there is a condition placed upon it, then it cannot be love. Love exists without conditions. When I am at peace, I notice that love is there. It always has been there and always will be. I just have to be still enough to notice.

It was in this room that I first experienced an unexpected moment of peace, one that uncovered the presence of love. Standing at the window and watching the dawn unfold, I saw a family of quail, several adults and at least 10 chicks, scurry out from underneath a flowering bougainvillea bush just outside the window. The quail were at my feet only inches away on the other side of the glass. The adults were beautifully marked—plumed topknots with bright russet heads and black faces, cream-colored bellies and russet wings flecked with white. I could see each feather and look into each eye.

I whispered for Patsy to come into the room. We stood together, my arm around her shoulders and hers around my waist, holding each other as the quail gathered at our feet. I cannot recall having any particular thoughts. There was no sense of "I." Looking at what I'd seen many times before, I could truly see what was there for the first time. They were incredibly beautiful. A miracle. In that peaceful moment, there was only a sense of gratitude and the presence of love. An open mind creates an open heart.

A feeling of gratitude and love is how I experience being totally present. Michael Brown wrote in *The Presence Process* that "...present moment awareness is not only a *state* of Being; it is a *Being*. Present moment awareness is, indeed, 'a Presence.' The Being and the state of Being have revealed themselves to me to be One and the same. By entering It, one becomes It. Present moment awareness is, therefore, a state of becoming. It is awareness embracing its fullest potential."

That is my experience—one of *becoming*. I am becoming more frequently present, awake and aware of a state of Being and The Being. With my self-concepts quieted and out of the way, my mind is at peace. This is not a giddy sense of bliss or rapture. It is plainly and simply a state of love, appreciation and gratitude. It is a state I create in meditation. It is a state I create as I relate with others and especially as I coach, which for me is a higher form of conscious meditation.

I've thought about what led me to that place with those people on that particular day at that exact time after a meandering walk through the streets of Los Angeles. Left. Right. Straight. Never backtracking. Was it a random series of turns and street crossings that got me there? A mere coincidence? I love the sense of wonder and awe the questions provoke. How wonderful it is to be alive and not have to know, yet trust I will understand when it is time to know. It is a part of becoming.

I can remember how as a child I wondered about the future. Who would I be? A success? A failure? Strong? Weak? Healthy? As a teen, the future was always an exciting concept, yet filled with mystery and anticipation. As an executive, I believed my job was to create a future for the organization. It looked like cause and effect. Think. Take action. Produce a result. If you like the result, do more. If not, do something else. Create the future. Isn't that the way it works?

Looking back at the most significant events in my life, I can easily question that. My most exciting transitions all seemed to transcend cause and effect. More than thirty years ago I walked through a doorway I had never seen before. Behind that door and across the room sat a beautiful young woman, Patsy, who became my wife and life partner. Our children were both conceived in unanticipated moments of love and passion. What delightfully surprising miracles they were and are today!

It's as if I've been on a path. A conversation with my father; a face in the jungle; years of reckless and irresponsible behavior followed by years of discipline, service and leadership. One seemingly random event leading to the next and then to the next bringing me to where I am today. Albert Einstein suspected that there was a natural order in the universe that lies hidden and spent most of his life seeking a glimpse of it. After all his work and study, he found that his science required faith in the inner harmony of the world. I share that faith in a natural order.

I started this book by sharing how at the airport I was struck by the sudden realization that I had lived a life without purpose, like a leaf in a stream being carried by the current. Now I see that I am being carried by a current and that purpose presents itself in every moment. It seems to be the natural order of things. I don't control the current. I don't choose the circumstances and the opportunities that are presented to me, but I do choose my intent and how I respond. I am given a choice in every moment to either act or not act. The more present I am the more apparent the choice becomes. It's as if there is no choice. There is only to do and to serve.

On different occasions this year, I've heard at least three people reference Einstein's quote: *"I think the most important question facing humanity is, 'Is the universe a friendly place?' This is the first and most basic question all people must answer for themselves."* Einstein saw how a society that thought about that question would predict how they would use their technology, science and natural resources—to either destroy all that was unfriendly, or if judged friendly then "...to create tools and models for understanding that universe. Because power and safety will come through understanding its workings and its motives."

Clearly, the same holds true for us as well. We must answer the question for ourselves. The more that I question my stressful thoughts, the more peace I find. The more peaceful my mind, the more power I access, the safer I feel and the freer I am to act. Jed McKenna who writes about enlightenment issued the challenge to "...think for yourself and figure out what's true. Ask yourself what's true until you know. It cannot be simpler; *you* are asleep and *you* can wake up."

All the transitions in this book, and in your life as you examine it, are variations on that transition from sleep to waking up. And as I awaken, I am finding a very friendly universe.

ROBERT D. REED PUBLISHERS ORDER FORM

Call in your order for fast service and quantity discounts
(541) 347-9882

OR order on-line at www.rdrpublishers.com using PayPal.
OR order by mail: Make a copy of this form; enclose payment information:
Robert D. Reed Publishers
1380 Face Rock Drive, Bandon, OR 97411
Note: Shipping is $3.50 1st book + $1 for each additional book.

Send indicated books to:

Name _____

Address_____

City _____ State _____ Zip _____

Phone _____ Fax_____ Cell _____

E-Mail _____

Payment by check /__/ or credit card /__/ *(All major credit cards are accepted.)*

Name on card _____

Card Number_____

Exp. Date _____ Last 3-Digit number on back of card _____

Qty.

The Secret of Transitions: How to Move Effortlessly to
Higher Levels of Success by James Manton .... $14.95 _____

100 Ways to Create Wealth
by Steve Chandler & Sam Beckford .... $24.95 _____

Customer Astonishment
by Darby Checketts................................... $14.95 _____

The Six-Figure Speaker: Formula for a Six-Figure Income as a
Professional Speaker by Cathleen Fillmore .... $19.95 _____

Handling Employment BS
by Geoffrey Hopper .... $19.95 _____

Ten Commitments for Building High Performance Teams
by Tom Massey....................................... $11.95 _____

Other book title(s) from website:

_____ $ _____

_____ $ _____